radical compassion

radical compassion

FINDING CHRIST IN THE HEART OF THE POOR

GARY SMITH, S.J.

LOYOLA PRESS.
A JESUIT MINISTRY
Chicago

LOYOLA PRESS.
A JESUIT MINISTRY

3441 N. Ashland Avenue
Chicago, Illinois 60657
(800) 621-1008
www.loyolapress.com

Scripture quotations are from the Jerusalem Bible © by Darton, Longman & Todd, Ltd., and Doubleday & Company, Inc. 1966, 1967, and 1968. Reprinted by permission.

The quotation on p. 23 by the U.S. bishops is from the United States Conference of Catholic Bishops' Office of Social Development and World Peace, Homelessness and Housing: A Human Tragedy, a Moral Challenge (Washington, D.C.: United States Conference of Catholic Bishops, 1988), 3.

The quotations on p. 57 by Jon Sobrino are from "Rich and Poor Churches and the Compassion Principle," in David Fleming, S.J., ed., A Spirituality for Contemporary Life: The Jesuit Heritage (St. Louis, Mo.: Review for Religious, 1991), 50.

The excerpt on p. 67 from "God's Grandeur" is from Gerard Manley Hopkins, *Poems and Prose of Gerard Manley Hopkins* (London: Penguin Classics, 1953), 2.

The excerpt on p. 104 from "Prayer" is from Lynn Martin, *Blue Bowl* (Yakima, Wash.: Blue Begonia Press, 2000), 27. Used by permission of the author.

The quotation on p. 110 by Abraham Heschel is from Samuel H. Dresner, ed., *I Asked for Wonder: A Spiritual Anthology* (New York: Crossroad, 1997), 46.

The story about Wells on pp. 179–183 originally appeared in the *National Catholic Reporter,* 16 October 1998, as "Unassuming 'Roofers' and Extraordinary Acts" by Gary Smith.

Interior design by Kathy Kikkert

Library of Congress Cataloging-in-Publication Data
Smith, Gary, S.J.
  Radical compassion : finding Christ in the heart of the poor / Gary Smith.
    p. cm.
  ISBN-13: 978-0-8294-2000-5
  ISBN-10: 0-8294-2000-2
  1. Church work with the poor--Catholic Church. 2. Church work with the poor--Oregon--Portland. 3. Poverty--Religious aspects--Catholic Church. I. Title.
  BX2347.8.P66 S65 2002
  261.8'325--dc21

Printed in the United States
            14 15 Bang 10 9 8 7

for the unsung

contents

chapter one

PEOPLE WITH NOTHING

TO PROVE:

LIVING AMONG THE POOR

I write this book so that the reader will have a
better understanding of the poor.

One morning I went to the
hotel room of Stewart, a thirty-five-year-old man who suffers from
cerebral palsy, which has disabled an arm and a leg and his sight.

Stewart has lived in single-room occupancy hotels (SROs) since
he left home in his twenties. His is a grungy looking room, needing a paint job. It has a small bathroom, a bed, a set of drawers for
his clothes, and a tiny half-kitchen. The door leads out to the long
and gloomy second-floor hallway of a four-story building. The
window looks out onto a bleak inner court.

I had come to help him get ready for a doctor's appointment,
and he talked as I helped him undress and get into the shower.

"I have this dumb disease, in this stupid body," he slowly told
me, "which I hate."

The smallest tasks of this young man's daily life are the tortured efforts of time and concentration: unbuttoning a shirt, drinking a cup of coffee, unlocking a door, crossing a street. As I helped him dry off and dress, we chatted about our lives and our families.

"How many brothers do you have, Garibaldi?" he asked, using his nickname for me. "Are you married? What did you have for breakfast?"

"Two brothers, Studebaker," I replied, using my name for him, "and a sister. No, I am not married, and I didn't eat breakfast."

His speech reflects longings and deprivations in his life. He told me of his twin: "He looks like me, but he is normal."

Stewart has an unaffected candor. As a matter of fact, he has no idea what it means to be pretentious. What you see is what you get. If he is happy, it is all there; if he is sad, one has no doubt.

That is often the way for people with no power, no money, no exterior beauty. They have nothing to prove. And so Stewart is nonthreatening. He crashes through my defenses. He brings out what is good, whole, and deep down in me: the ability to love tenderly, speak truthfully, receive openly, and face gently my own weaknesses.

■ ■ ■

On my way to work every day, I walk down Third Street in Portland, in a section of the city called Old Town, through a scene played out in the poor areas of every large city in the United States: the unemployed looking for work; drug dealers furtively hawking their heroin, cocaine, and methamphetamines; residents from the many SROs moving in and out of their buildings; burned-out alcoholics coming off or beginning another day of panhandling and drinking and misery; addicts engaging in the endless hunt for another fix; lines of people waiting to get food or clothes or shelter;

the occasional nervous and fatigued prostitute wandering by; individuals talking incoherently to themselves; staff persons from a variety of agencies going about their work; alert police slowly surveying the streets on foot, on bikes, in cars.

All this activity takes place in an area comprising low-income SROs, a Salvation Army facility that feeds and houses the poor, a couple of rescue missions that also run drug rehab programs, storefront operations that come and go depending on money and interest, vacant buildings retained by speculators waiting for the economic boom to swallow Old Town, dark and dreary taverns, city-run shelters, parking lots that are full in the day and empty at night, a nonprofit restaurant that serves the needy of Old Town, a women's drop-in center, Outreach Ministry, a strip joint, an adult bookstore, and a community police station. Creeping into all of this, as Portland's economic prosperity asserts itself, are upscale coffee shops, some high-priced restaurants and mom-and-pop grocery stores, and SROs that are being converted into condos.

I live in the middle of it all in a room in the Downtown Chapel of St. Vincent de Paul Church. I wear several hats in terms of my ministry: working part-time for Outreach Ministry in Burnside (OMB), a money-management and personal care agency; assisting the Macdonald Center, a social outreach arm of the chapel, with SRO work; ministering to inmates at the county justice center; and hanging out on the streets.

On occasion I come across a young flutist in the downtown commercial area of Portland. He is an Ichabod Crane of a man, wiry and fragile, and looks as if he is made of broomsticks and baling wire. He is usually wearing baggy pants and a raggedy sweatshirt. His full head of hair flies in a dozen different directions, especially on a windy day. There is a beat-up old hat at his feet containing a few coins from appreciative fans. His entire self is absorbed in the furious tooting on his cheap wooden instrument.

Coming closer, one hears a strange thing: he's playing nonsense notes. No melody. No organized rhythm. The listener experiences incomprehensible music and the mysterious force that propels those flying fingers. The musician never seems to stop, lost in and driven by the inner power of some mysterious melody. He looks straight ahead, apparently oblivious to gawkers like me.

I linger for a few minutes whenever I see him. Inevitably I have created an imaginary scenario between us in which I approach Mr. Flutist and point out the obvious: "Excuse me, sir, are you aware that your music is not making any sense?"

He drops the flute from his lips, eyes me, and says, with a hint of exasperation, "So what? I'm crazy. But, man, I've got to play my song. I mean, don't you?"

This book is about my song. It is not all the music in me, but there is a lot of it here. It is a song primarily about the people with whom I have lived and worked over the past several years as part of my mission on the streets as a priest in the Society of Jesus, the Jesuits. I have changed most of their names, but their stories, their compelling stories, I could never change. I have tried to express how they have broken me open and helped me to understand my own heart, and how they have led me closer to the song of hope for all human beings, which is in the heart of God.

I write this book so that the reader will have a better understanding of the poor. I write it, too, to keep out in front of me a fundamental chord in my song: that the church, when it becomes poor and internalizes the suffering of the poor, understands compassion and the demands of justice. The just and compassionate church becomes the incarnation of the heart and song of Christ.

chapter two

COCKROACHES, CONVERSATION, AND COLLECTORS: INSIDE THE SROS

> In the midst of one-way conversations, I am communicating all the time. I try to affirm this human being, so lost in his own world of memories, bitter and sweet.

There is in me a longing to be real, to be authentic, to be a clear reflection of what my heart holds at its deepest levels. It is a goal that the gospel steadfastly holds up as an invitation to me, to the church. It is when the church embraces the gospel selflessly that it bears the heart of God and becomes real to the world. And when it is real, the church makes God believable.

This truth is the impelling force behind the ministry of the St. Vincent de Paul Downtown Chapel, where I live. The chapel sponsors a social service outreach program, in which I participate, out of a facility called the Macdonald Center. Macdonald Center takes its two-person teams of staff and volunteers into the forty-plus single-room occupancy hotels in the Old Town/downtown Portland area. There in the SROs, within the confines of the small rooms, the teams spend time visiting with people who have limited, if any, contact with the outside world.

Like the dirt and concrete pockets under the Portland bridges or the recessed doorways on Skid Row, these rooms are the nooks and crannies of the city's poor and near homeless, and frequently, they are the spawning grounds of paralyzing feelings of separation and loneliness. Paradoxically, the darkness of such places is light for the church, because there the church is invited and challenged to claim what is best in itself: the ability to love compassionately, to serve unselfishly, to profess and speak to what is truthful.

■ ■ ■

I was in a hotel this afternoon, carrying on one of those endless conversations with Ned, who tells the same story over and over to anyone who will listen. He might as well play a cassette. That is, if he lets you in his room.

Ned is in his late seventies, one of those rare birds who has lived that long in spite of pounding down a fifth of vodka a day and complementing his drinking with a couple packs of cigarettes.

While he was in the middle of his monologue, a cockroach appeared, laboriously climbing up the wall behind him. It was huge; in fact, it was so huge that it couldn't retain its adhesion to the wall, and about a quarter of the way up, it crashed to the floor. It followed this cycle repeatedly: climbing the wall, falling off, and beginning its bloated way back up again. Sort of a metaphor for Ned's stories.

He regaled me once again with tales of his lost family and of how his two sons had dumped him ("It's all their fault"), of the crackpots in his hotel ("Why do they let nuts like that in here?"), and of his World War II exploits.

Such conversations take place in the confines of these obscure little rooms. These encounters are the essence of the ministry of presence. In the midst of one-way conversations, I am communicating all the time. I try to affirm this human being, so lost in his own world of memories, bitter and sweet. I could try to preach religion to the shut-in, but it would be like talking about high-speed particle physics. And even if I did, he or she would, one way or another, show me to the door.

No, I bide my time and wait, trying to pace them in their conversation, believing that in the presence of my brand of love they will discover within themselves the capacity to uncover that inner spirit that has been buried under bad decisions, bitterness, booze, and dizzying loneliness. And I don't say this with condescension or superiority. I've experienced that presence of love myself, and in that presence I have grown, even when I had built some barbed-wire fences around myself. I trust that my way of being present to Ned will be used by God.

■ ■ ■

One of the factors of SRO life is cockroaches. If you don't like being distracted while having a conversation, try talking fairly serious stuff in an SRO, where roaches run up the walls or crawl out from underneath coat collars.

Many SRO residents throughout Old Town have been awakened by their smoke alarms, triggered not by smoke but by a roach looking for a dark and cozy home. Roll over, go back to sleep. No fire; it's just a roach.

Sometimes I get a sense of how long someone has lived in a particular room by the condition of the smashed roaches on the wall:

fresh wall kill means the resident has recently moved in; petrified wall kill translates into a veteran occupant. One becomes an amateur archaeologist with a specialty in cockroaches.

Robert's roaches always were in a herd around a hot-water pipe at its junction with the ceiling. He even had names for some of them and could identify them as they wandered off in solitary fashion across the walls of his dingy, dirty SRO room. I knew another guy who named his roaches after Old Testament prophets.

One old fellow we visit has legions of the things, in all sizes, scurrying and surveying as they traverse tables, bed, walls, clothes, food. There are even scouts moving along the bed on which he sits day in and day out. He keeps a piece of paper tightly rubber-banded around his pipe—stem and bowl—to keep them out.

When I was a community organizer in Oakland, California, one of the first cases I tackled involved a woman with a serious roach problem living in an east Oakland neighborhood. On either side of her residence were speculator-owned vacant houses. She nearly gassed herself to death with Raid because the roaches from the vacant houses were invading her home like army ants. The owner of those vacant houses couldn't have cared less, even after written complaints and phone calls. Then he was invited to a neighborhood meeting to rectify the situation, under the threat—if he refused—of bringing half the neighborhood to his residence with an abundant supply of bottled roaches. Naturally, the neighborhood organization assured him, Raid would be provided free of charge.

The politics of cockroaches is one that always forces the poor to lead the charge. Why is it so hard for hotel owners to regularly attend to the problem of roaches? And how much should one complain? Same point could be made for mice or rats. Why should people who spend more than a third of their income for housing— housing that is often poor and code defiant—not be protected from property owners who are indifferent to health hazards?

Of course, roaches will always be with us. Ditto for rats, lice, and mice. Such creatures will always have a foothold in poor areas, but that is no excuse for not endeavoring to keep the problem under control. In some cases nothing is done to rectify the situation because the owners are greedy, and the poor have little power.

■ ■ ■

Gene rolled toward me in his wheelchair. He is a fifty-three-year-old man, battling cancer and diabetes. He is a Vietnam vet but doesn't like to talk about that "bleeping war." Underneath his wisdom and an amazing amount of cheerfulness, I can feel his anger.

In a strange story, he laughingly told me of the day of great "Christmas cheer." He was trying to make a little extra money, so he got a job as a Salvation Army bell ringer in front of a local department store. While he was ringing away, his colostomy bag broke. He said he was assisted to the emergency room by one of the folks who regularly dumped money into the pot. He was laughing about it all because he never returned to his station and had not a clue what might have happened to the money. For sure, he won't be seeing any of it, and he doubted that he would be hired again.

With Gene off to other things, I ran into John, who was into another devastating drunk. I am always astonished by the amount of drinking that people can do and still live. John is a case in point.

In contrast to the optimistic viewpoint of humanity that Gene has, John told me that "some rip-off car tow man" tried to charge him 150 bucks for the overnight tow of his car off a lot, after the lot owner had told John that he could leave his car (an Olympic-class clunker) on the lot for two days. John said that his anger forced the tow man to back down, and he was charged only a hundred dollars. So there was John telling me the story, walking with me down the hotel hallway, his arm draped over my shoulder. It was amusing to hear him say, "No way was I going to let that guy fuck with me."

Sure, John, yet you got so mad that you proceeded to drink yourself silly.

He bade me good-bye and ducked into his room.

■ ■ ■

At the end of the hallway I ran into skin-and-bones Maureen. I asked her what was happening, although I knew she was drugging and tricking. She talked vaguely about going into rehab that week. It was strange, because she had been on my mind and in my prayers lately. I reminded her of her two children and that she would never get them back if she didn't start rehabilitation. I don't like to dump guilt on anyone, but I did want a voice of love and responsibility to find its way into her murky and fuzzy-brained world. And she knows, as much as she hates it, that my voice is true and one that she can trust. Isn't this the saddest part of drugs: that mommas can forget their children?

Ironically, she informed me that Mick, a mutual friend, overdosed last week in Seattle. It was deliberate, she said. He propped himself up by a tree overlooking Lake Washington and fired away. There were two empty needles, one of which was still in his arm. She must know that this could happen to her, too. Yet I am afraid that even this will not deter her. It is madness.

■ ■ ■

Joe, a shut-in at an SRO, is a seventyish former lumber worker. I greeted him in his room, and he remained in bed during my short stay.

I always pride myself on observing what is in someone's room, and today I noted the usual mess: the toaster at the end of his bed that doubles as a foot warmer; dirty clothes; empty beer cans; an electric frying pan containing fermenting fried potatoes; a lipstick message on his mirror that read, "I love you, Joe"; two *Playboy* foldouts hanging lopsided on the walls; and, of course, the omnipresent cockroaches.

Joe informed me that he was still planning to check into the VA treatment center in White City if he could save enough money from his next pension check. As I was wondering if he ever got out of bed, I realized that there, underneath the shabby blanket, was another person. He had a prostitute with him.

I mumbled something about returning later. He said, "Yeah, Father, that would be better."

So much for the crack observer, Father Smith.

■ ■ ■

Thanksgiving and Christmas holidays are always a paradox on the streets and in the SROs. On the one hand, there is a glut of food: free turkey dinners, huge boxes of food, and a little army of do-gooders who drive around handing out bags of groceries in blissful incomprehension of the world they have temporarily entered. On the other hand, there is always the clinging isolation that permeates Old Town like a fungus: people who have no family and few, if any, friends, facing the holiday in dreadful apprehension.

For several Thanksgivings, I loaded up two Styrofoam containers with turkey and mashed potatoes, prepared by the chapel kitchen staff, and walked them over to Willie's apartment. It was too difficult for him to come to the dining room, where there was a big feed for seniors in the area.

Willie was in his sixties, a recovering alcoholic, and a veteran of decades of drinking and riding the rails after he left his native Missouri. He had lived in the same SRO for fifteen years.

Willie's room was a mess in an ordered kind of way. He hung his few clothes from a nail on the tobacco-stained walls and located canned food items on an open shelf. Half of his sheetless bed was full of paperback Westerns and three clock radios, and the other half, where he slept, contained nothing but the saggy outline of his chunky little body, shaped by fifteen years of Willie use. Hanging on the walls and from his bedposts was an assortment of wrist-watches, twenty-one of them. He used to tell me that it was better to collect cheap watches than to drink.

I always enjoyed our meal together. Willie would sit and gum his food down as we talked about our usual topics: the weather, his family in the Midwest, a program he had seen on TV, or the latest Louis L'Amour book that he was reading. He didn't get out much, because he was a consummate introvert and because arthritic knees limited his range of walking. Willie was simple, good, always hospitable and welcoming. Invariably he asked about my sister, Susan, who had visited Willie with me when she was in town. Both former alcoholics, they swapped horror stories. He remained always solicitous for her health.

Shortly after I met him, I noticed all the cash he had on his bedside table. I discovered that he was draining his savings account but wasn't putting anything back into it. When I asked him why he wasn't depositing the cash from his monthly Supplemental Security Income checks, he said he just hadn't gotten around to it. It turns out that he had three thousand dollars hidden around his room. He didn't even know he had that much money.

I wound up walking the bundle of cash over to the bank, nervous about having that much money on my body. I felt as though I was wearing a sandwich sign like the ones that read, "Eat at

Joe's," only mine read "Rob me." One of the baffling mysteries of this episode is why the hotel predators had never walked in on him, beaten him up, and walked off with at least the watches. That much money in an SRO is a fortune.

Eventually a hernia operation did Willie in. I received a phone call at three o'clock one morning from his former hotel manager who always looked after him; Willie had died in his sleep at the foster home where he was recuperating. I spoke to one of his sisters by phone later in the day. Within the week, his ashes were sent back to his two sisters in his little Missouri hometown, and he was buried in the family plot.

What was Willie for me? Most of all, he kept me simple: no proselytizing, no intellectualizing, no need to impress, nothing to prove. He accepted me for who I was, probably a lot better than I did him. I wear one of his watches. His sisters gave it to me. It was Willie's wish that I have it.

■ ■ ■

Macdonald Center staffer Mara and I, visiting one day at a run-down SRO hotel, met Billie, one of the most winsome eccentrics I have ever encountered. He was in his thirties, had a head full of blond tousled hair and thoughtful, darting eyes, and was full of engaging hospitality. He traveled on the roads all the time, so there was never much in his room. Only one thing stood out: a large sketchbook and half a dozen or so pencils.

He was a wheel of energy, an endless talker who motored along at a furious speed but was self-effacing in a conscious and haphazard way ("I know I talk too much and bore people"). In the distant past of his life's long march, there had been struggles with mental illness, family conflicts, fights in which he had been severely beaten up, sexual abuse in prisons, and an unceasing compulsion to travel.

Periodically his angry paranoia would surface, and he would revile and scold individuals in the government and in corporations. Similar kinds of meandering endless diatribes were directed toward his wicked stepsister.

Over the months he often referred to me as Robin Hood because he felt that I was concerned about people like him. And he always made a special effort to be sensitive and modest around Mara. He also began to show us some of his sketches, which were frequently of human beings, finely detailed. They made me think of drawings I had seen in a volume on Michelangelo.

"I draw a lot because it helps me to slow down my mind. It goes so fast, so endlessly. I guess that is a symptom of my mental illness."

In the course of the few months I knew him, Billie said these things about himself with the openness and directness that characterized all his conversations with Mara and me:

I am a good guy.
I am lonely.
I am crazy.
I am bipolar.
I am without friends by choice.
I am gentle.
I am angry and pissed off.
I am a compulsive talker who feels like he sometimes abuses the
     listener with all the talk.
I am like a little bunny in the woods.
I am safe with Mother Nature; she won't hurt me.
I am a victim of a baseball bat attack to my head.
I have been butt-fucked in prison.
I am treated—to the point of grief—inhumanely, indifferently,
     and cruelly by Social Security bureaucrats.

I am longing to know a woman.
I am an artist.
I am a friend of squirrels.
I will be stupid for the rest of my life.

In one of our last visits, just before he left town, the irrepressible Billie said to me: "You, Gary, are like the feeling I had when I took out the last distasteful pimento in a salad my mom had made. Everything was then okay to eat and enjoy. When you arrive, Gary Robin Hood, everything is okay."

Whenever I left his room, I felt the same way about being around him.

■ ■ ■

Moving through a couple of the hotels this afternoon, I was struck by how the deprivations that people experience can lead to eccentric kinds of compensation—like the hoarding syndrome of some of the poor. For example, Raymond receives a dollar a day from his money manager. He never spends it. He has a wallet bulging with ones. It looks as though he is carrying a bloated brown beaver in his back pocket. Paul lives in a fourteen-by-ten room. He is a self-professed dumpster diver—has been since the beginning of time. His apartment is a warehouse of goodies: furniture, clothes, hubcaps, discarded city traffic signs, broken toys, magazines stacked against the wall. There are rumors that he has hand grenades buried in his room, a kind of dynamite in that meadow of stuff. "They are in his pile of radio parts," one insider told me.

One collector woman hoarded clothes. She was probably a physically beautiful person before age, mental illness, and abusive men had exacted their price. She had so many boxes of clothes in her room that they took over, like an insatiable octopus. Boxes, reaching to the ceiling, controlled the approach to the bathroom, blocked off the windows, filled her bed, stuffed her closet. Those damn boxes controlled everything from where she slept to her sex life. Someday, of course, the clothes will make her beautiful again. Her obvious conclusion: keep them.

Some individuals squirrel huge amounts of food in their rooms, like, well, squirrels. They walk away from parties and free-food centers with a dinner in their tummies and ham sandwiches in their coat pockets. Often the food becomes nothing more than a glorious meal for delighted roaches and mice. One woman cannot pass up anything on the street. Her room is full of newspapers, gum wrappers, cigarette butts, and street garbage. Wilson must have fifty pairs of pants in his room. Barney collects televisions; some work, some don't. He has four sets that get only one channel. Horace, a voracious reader, has jammed his room with science-fiction paperbacks that he has ripped off from the local free library.

Things give meaning to the lives of people who are deprived of authentic human contact. It is not necessarily a quirk of the poor: the millionaire builds an ostentatious house; the CEO wears a Rolex; the politician has a few people in his pocket; the dictator has his disposable private army; the preacher surrounds herself with unread theology books. Collecting things fills gaps in our hearts and gives expression to an internalized deprivation from the past.

■ ■ ■

Macdonald Center staffer Melissa and I were in a hotel recently to see Ronald. Roly-poly and sixty years old, Ronald was plain and poor. He had spent most of his life in the midst of or on the edges of mental illness. His life had been a landscape dotted with mental institutions, community mental health facilities, cheap hotels, and empty, friendless moments. As a child he lost an eye in a scissors accident and in addition was plagued by a hearing deficiency; both were factors that, in combination with his illness, had diminished his opportunities to learn the normal social skills that most of us take for granted. As a result, he was shy, nervous, uncertain, and in need of medication every day to control the mental illness.

Yet Ronald had the capacity to engage people—once he trusted them. His honesty and contagious sense of humor were qualities that Melissa and I cherished. He liked to paint watercolors, and a few of his letter-sized works were always thumbtacked to the plain white wall. They offset the aching sparseness of his room: a bed with a drawer underneath for his few articles of clothing, a radio on a small table, a washing sink, a chair, and a closet. He once gave Melissa a painting he called *Root Canal*. His other big love was *Popular Mechanics* magazine, the only reading material I ever saw in his room.

During one visit we asked Ronald if we could have a small celebration for his birthday and my birthday, both of which had occurred a few weeks earlier. We would bring the cake. "Yes, that would be fine," he said.

But we weren't sure he would be in his room when we came; sometimes he forgot about our visits and went out for a walk and a smoke.

But we lucked out; Ronald was in. Was he ever. There he stood, ready as a sentinel, his good eye gleaming back at us, dressed for the occasion in a brilliant red polo shirt and wearing an understated smile that betrayed his excitement. Pushed up against the window, which overlooked Burnside Avenue, was his table, set with shiny red plastic dishes, knives, forks, paper cups, and white napkins. The napkins, on closer inspection, turned out to be neatly folded toilet paper.

Somewhere in his hotel he had dug up two extra chairs. He had spent his limited allowance (a local mental health agency was his payee) not only on the tableware. He had also splurged on a quart of chocolate ice cream, two huge bottles of root beer and cream soda, and three chocolate muffins. Between Melissa's cake, Ronald's chunky muffins, the ice cream, the soda pop, and some killer whipped cream, we stuffed ourselves silly.

It was the party of the century. We were in the presence of un-yielding simplicity and care. He who had so little was giving us a lesson in how to give, and with not one hint of self-absorption. He was loving us in the best way he could.

The surprises continued. Three-quarters of the way through the party, Ronald handed me a tiny package, wrapped in lined writing paper and Scotch tape. "Here's your birthday present, Gary." Inside the package was a leather coin purse that he had fashioned himself with tools provided at the mental health center. Turning the coin purse over in my hands, I was speechless. When Melissa and I left the hotel that afternoon, we were like two kids who had stumbled upon some grand treasure in the forest.

Not long afterward, Ronald was diagnosed with cancer and began an aggressive treatment of radiation and chemotherapy. It was only a short time before the whole process wore his body down. Near the end, we talked in the nursing home about death, but it was never a concern for him. He didn't ponder things much beyond the moment, and I mean that in the most praiseworthy way. He was a pure and loving little man who had lived his life with a mountain of handicaps. And in spite of a million reasons for living in self-pity, he had within him—every day—the amazing ca-pacity to make coin purses and share his soda pop with others.

One morning I received the phone call from the nursing home. Ronald had died in the night. That night, after the smoke from the day had cleared, I prayed in the chapel for him, commending him to God and giving thanks for the blessing of his life. Ronald touched my heart because he would not allow my sophistication to impede his truth and goodness.

> *No, it was to shame the wise that God chose what is foolish by human reckoning . . . ; those whom the world thinks common and contemptible are the ones that God has chosen—those who are nothing at all to show up those who are everything.*
> 1 CORINTHIANS 1:27–28

■ ■ ■

Clyde was a potbellied gnome of a man with a balding head and a round, round face. He usually wore a cowboy hat, either one that had been given to him or the occasional hat he had found while dumpster diving for cans. When I first met him, while visiting residents at one of the SROs, he was pushing sixty. He came originally from Oklahoma and had spent most of his life riding the rails and working odd jobs. Along the way his health broke (as he would say, "It wasn't the years; it was the miles"), and he received Supplemental Security Income. He had never had a formal education, but he was never lacking for words, which he uttered in his delicious good-ole-boy drawl. He drank his beer out of one of the grimiest coffee mugs I have ever seen.

The man was raised as a Pentecostal, and in spite of the fact that he could barely read, he referred to and quoted from the New Testament as well as any Scripture scholar. Sometimes he would make reference to a chapter and verse of the Bible that had nothing to do with the subject at hand, but it gave him the occasion to launch into some theological truth. After he found out that I was a Catholic priest, he became my self-appointed teacher in an effort to make a preacher out of me. If Clyde saw me as he trudged along the streets, pushing a grocery cart loaded with redeemable bottles and cans, he would typically hail me with "Hey, preacher, come here. I've got something to tell you."

Those times when he would instruct me in his sparsely furnished apartment were special moments. One day he said, "You know, Preacher Man, you got to get this about the Holy Ghost if you're going to be a preacher. You got to have the Holy Ghost if you are going to cure addicts. And you got to beg God for it."

"Is it that simple, Clyde? I just have to lay my hands on someone and ask the Holy Ghost to help me?"

"Well, of course it is, if you got the Holy Ghost. But you got to realize that man can't heal a fly, only God. You need to lock yourself in a closet for forty days if you want to get the Holy Ghost. And then, after that kind of prayer, if you see some woman lying down dying of stomach cancer, you got to look down on her and say, 'Woman, get yourself up and go get yourself a hot dog and eat it.'"

"Well, why don't you spend more time preaching and healing on the streets, Clyde? It's clear you've got the Holy Ghost."

"No, I don't," he replied. "I am a backslider. Now read Acts 2, first thirteen verses. And listen!"

I read from his well-underlined Bible, and as I plowed through it, he would nod in approval, his eyes closed, as he puffed on a fat, poorly rolled cigarette and made editorial comments on the passage. How many afternoons we engaged each other this way.

One day, when I was doing a memorial service in the lobby of his hotel, Clyde appeared on the stairs leading down from the second floor to the lobby. He knew the person who had died and asked if he could sing a song out of respect for the deceased. Clyde thereupon gave us a neck-tingling version of "Amazing Grace" in that raw Oklahoma accent. His love for singing old hymns flowed though him like the sun coming through the lobby window. His simplicity of faith, like so many of his instructions to me, left all of us, even the crusty old cynical veterans of that particular hotel, shaking our heads. I thought to myself, *Here is a man without guile.*

Once, while my visiting companion Fred and I were meeting with Clyde, I mentioned that Fred was going to Phoenix with his asthma-plagued wife in the hopes of relieving her illness. I asked Clyde if he would mind praying for Fred, and he moved to it without hesitation.

Laying his hands on Fred's head, he prayed something like this: "Lord, I know you love this woman and that you want her to be with you. But remember that this man loves her, too, and he needs her and she needs him and they need to be together. So give them some more time, even as you are healing her from her illness. Let them love each other as you love them."

How ironic it was. Here was Clyde, living with whatever pain from the past, denying that he had the "Holy Ghost."

After he became seriously ill with liver and heart problems, Clyde moved to a nursing home where I was able to see him only a few times. It was clear to me, after my first visit to the home, that he had charmed the facility's staff with his mix of kindness and earthy faith. His death came peacefully one night in the fall.

I have had a lot of teachers in the course of my life. For directness, selflessness, and utter belief in his student's destiny, he was the champ.

"Okay, Preacher Man, now read Isaiah 49, verse 2."

> *He made my mouth a sharp sword,*
> *and hid me in the shadow of his hand.*
> *He made me into a sharpened arrow,*
> *and concealed me in his quiver.*

. . .

I went over to see Robbie at his SRO. It is a hotel used by the county for those poor who are physically mobile but suffer from mental illness or forms of dementia that require a special residence. It is a gloomy place, however courageous and creative the staff may be. In the lobby, I walked through a gauntlet of silent, staring residents. It reminded me of nursing homes I have visited.

Robbie was in the first-floor smoking room, puffing away like a steam engine, fifty pounds down from the days before he began chemotherapy. I don't think he understands what is going on.

As we talked, we were periodically interrupted by the grunts and exclamations of an old gentleman who was shuffling in and out of the smoking room. The man moved like a robot, ambling back and forth in the room, making his noises, never looking at anyone, never saying anything. Robbie was unperturbed. He was so accustomed to the man that he would time his words to me around the sounds that regularly emanated from the old man.

What is it that eats away at me at this residence? It is the vulnerability and emotional nakedness of those who live out their lives here, sick and lonely, most out of hinge with life and society around them. They have few visitors, if any. In most cases, they have no family, and if they do have a family, it has probably dumped this member like an old book or an inconvenient memory. Being in this hotel is like being in a ward of orphaned babies; it is an environment of deprivation, with bleak prospects for the future. Coming here, notwithstanding my love for Robbie, is like a blow to the gut.

And yet each one of these people had a momma, and each presumably has a life story. But there is no one to whom they can tell the story, no one to carefully listen. How did this young man in front of Robbie and me, staring out the window, get here? Did that catatonic woman in front of the TV have any children? And the striking white-haired fellow, there, in the corner of the smoking room, does he have a family? Did he play ball and make love and throw rocks into the ocean? Did all at one time live with the hope that they might have what society judges to be most important and desirable in life: joy, love, a home, a good reputation, security in the world, and children to cherish their memory?

All these realizations fuel my energy to be present to Robbie, to give him the best of my attention, to treasure his story. He, and all these others, will not be forgotten.

■ ■ ■

> *Housing should not be treated as a commodity but as a basic human right that is grounded in our view of the human person and the responsibility of society to protect the life and dignity of every person by providing the conditions where human life and dignity are enhanced.*
>
> U.S. CATHOLIC CONFERENCE

Joseph and I go out for coffee once in a while; we have been doing so ever since we met one night in a free-food line. He suffers from a mental illness that involves severe spells of depression. He is supported by Supplemental Security Income (SSI), but he raids trash cans on a regular basis, retrieving soda and beer cans and redeeming them at the local supermarket. A few years ago he freaked out in his apartment, trashed it, and was subsequently evicted, which among others things resulted in a long-term loss of the rent subsidy provided him by the Department of Housing and Urban Development (HUD).

Presently he spends $350 of his $500 monthly SSI check on rent for a place that looks like a bat cave. He shares a toilet and shower with several other people on the same floor. He struggles financially, especially if he has to buy items that aren't basic necessities, like a lamp or a radio or a pair of shoes. It is unlikely that he will obtain a subsidized apartment any time soon, since he is on a new HUD waiting list, and the waiting period is eighteen to twenty-four months. And that is not just a Portland phenomenon; the waiting period is longer in other cities. He knows all this, which leads to more depression.

We walked down the street to our favorite cheap coffee shop, heading into a newly developed portion of the downtown area that ironically is not four blocks from where he lives and just about that distance from many low-income SROs. The new buildings that line the street contain condos that are selling for half a million dollars. Count them: five hundred thousand big, fat dollars. Recently a traditional low-income SRO hotel was sold and will be converted into condos that will be priced strictly for the wealthy.

People ask me where homeless people are coming from. Some of them have been squeezed out by the inexorable movement of real-estate capital into traditionally poor areas and can no longer afford what used to be affordable. The cycle serves to widen the gap between the rich and poor in Portland and in our country. It is an ominous sight and portends a future wherein individuals currently housed will become homeless.

There is something wrong. The reality of homelessness, inadequate housing, and the lack of affordable housing is a national disgrace. This reality undermines the life and dignity of so many of our brothers and sisters who lack a decent place to live. It destroys lives and families. The crime of homelessness is not that people live in filthy camps under bridges, or that families sleep illegally in their cars, or that the homeless and the near homeless panhandle. The crime is that homelessness exists. And the reason people are homeless or that people pay three-fourths of their income on housing is that there is not adequate affordable housing. It's nuts. How can a city countenance the development of off-the-charts-expensive condos and allow housing for the poor to diminish? How can politicians back tax cuts when the infrastructure of affordable housing is falling apart?

We must view and confront the diminution of affordable housing in light of the church's traditional view of housing. It is not a commodity, something to be bought and sold like a fancy car or a trip to the Caribbean; it is a basic human right. This right is grounded in the theological truth that every human being is created in God's image. If that right is denied, an injustice is being committed. Society has the responsibility to protect the life and dignity of every person by providing the conditions where that life and that dignity are not undermined.

The church has to take a stand, and it has to be indignant. It not only has to create its own affordable housing programs (just as surely as soup kitchens), but it also has to challenge greed-driven, land-gobbling institutions and the persons behind them. Like vultures, these same people feed off prime real estate in areas of traditional renter-occupied housing where only the poor can afford to live. As a result, the poor are squeezed out of their housing. The church in turn has to hound the government to deal with money-driven real-estate trusts that hungrily acquire property and cater to the housing needs of the rich. In short, the church must ensure that people are not denied their fundamental economic right to decent housing. And it has to fight those who, by their actions, scoff at that fundamental right.

The dialogue with our economic culture—and it has to be insistent—must be driven by our concern for the poor and vulnerable and those shorn of dignity because they do not have a place to live. Two-thirds of those who qualify for housing assistance in the United States cannot get it because it is not available.

Joseph and I had our coffee and noticed a sign in our coffee shop that said the little place was going out of business. The proprietor informed us that the rents in this particular building were being doubled. We will start looking around for another el cheapo coffee shop. Our prospects are diminishing.

chapter three

TALKING WITH MANNEQUINS:
MENTAL ILLNESS ON THE STREETS

My experience with the mentally ill on the streets
is that there is a place in them that is sacred,
and they can touch it in the presence of
one whom they can trust, a person committed
to walking with them through the minefields.

I went out for fresh air one recent
evening and walked past a young man who was engaged in a conversation with a mannequin in the display window of a large department store. It was as though he and the mannequin were
having coffee together: the disturbed guy making his points, his
fingers jabbing holes in the air, and the enigmatic, gazing mannequin, its slight come-hither smile egging him on.

People are talking to themselves all over the Burnside area—indeed, in every city I have ever been in. How does one wind up
talking to oneself or to an inanimate object? What is the breaking

point, how much illness must exist, how much pain and suffering must be endured before the intimate and precious part of ourselves becomes unmoored and floats away, making us incapable of normal human intercourse?

The anatomy of loneliness is a very visible one in the city. It's true, there are many mentally ill people whose inner processes drive them to a disconnection with the world around them, and one can only hope that medication and proper mental health facilities will assist them in their search for human connection. On the other hand, many individuals, I think, are driven to talking to themselves and to the mannequins of their lives because there is no one around to listen to them or care about them. They aren't mentally ill; they're just lonely. Some folks connect more with the cockroaches, mice, cats, dogs, birds, and plants in their SRO rooms than they do with other human beings. This is not so much by choice as it is a result of the poison of human disregard.

■ ■ ■

Lorna walked with me to jail and back this morning, waiting patiently while I was seeing people. She is full of wonderful one-liners, like "Why don't they serve communion to people on airplanes?" Today, she could not understand why the "almighty Creator" could not heal her of her inner conflicts, which involve voices in her head. She is very "pissed off" at Jesus.

"He could cure me if he wanted to," she said. "And so he allows me to be afflicted by these evil voices. I will suffer for him, but I do not like what he is doing."

A pretty honest reasoning, and the same one uttered by generations of people who, innocent as the air, find themselves bearing emotional and physical afflictions. As we walked down the final block before she headed toward her residence, she said to me, "You know, Gary, I am a greyhound dog in the chase for Jesus, the rabbit, but he always stays in front of me and I cannot reach him to be healed."

I told her that I thought Jesus was the greyhound and we are the rabbits and that, in fact, Jesus was present to her, but the healing she wanted was going to be accomplished in a way that neither one of us would understand.

■ ■ ■

Sam is a charming young man I met in the hotels. His schizophrenia began to show up when he was a teenager. The voices get so bad that he takes medication, which puts him in a sleeping mode for ten to twelve hours a day. Often he leaves his radio and TV running so that they will deflect the internal noise. He is a man of friendly disposition who thinks just about everything is great. If it isn't, it soon will be.

I asked him, as I always do when I make my weekly visit to his room, how his battle with the voices is going. He frequently says that they have been quiet for almost a week, although occasionally one sneaks in a little whispering campaign over something that can't wait.

He told me recently, almost casually, as though he was describing what he had for breakfast, "I had to call the cops on my voices the other day because they were really bugging me."

"What did they say?" I asked him.

Sam: "They told me to see my doctor."

Me: "Did you?"

Sam: "No, I'll run it past him next week at our regular appointment."

■ ■ ■

Most literature on mental illness and homelessness indicates that more than half of the people on the streets are mentally ill with manifestations of the following, to name a few: affective disorders; schizophrenia, in all its many variations; recurrent depressive and manic-depressive disorders (bipolarism); post-traumatic stress disorder; borderline personality disorders; paranoid and delusional thinking; mental retardation; brain disorders and sickness brought on by drug and alcohol addiction; sociopathic behavior; and forms of senility and dementia. Thirty percent of the mentally ill compound their problems with substance abuse.

Some of those who suffer from mental illness and are poor or homeless are often too disabled to take advantage of the welfare safety nets and local shelters. At least, that is my perception of it. Every day I see many signs of this truth. Some people are walking the streets or sitting around hallucinating. Some are terribly old; others are painfully young. Some look lost and disoriented; others are making a beeline for an imaginary important meeting. I have seen the mentally ill sleeping on heating grates, on park benches, and underneath bridges. And I have known some who, overcome by the dark impulses of their illness, have slipped into an endless spiral of chaos and have killed themselves.

The percentages above are consistent with the population that lives in the SROs of Old Town. And there is high turnover of residence for those who are ill. It is not uncommon for a mentally ill person to reside—within a few years—in apartments, community residences, board and care facilities, homeless shelters, psychiatric wards, nursing homes, and motels. The reason is that the illness creates such frequent disruptive mental processes that the person is unable to perform the normal tasks involved in maintaining a residence: minimal personal hygiene, care for the housing, management of money. Throw in a lack of certain social skills and there is further erosion of self-sufficiency, self-care, self-direction, interpersonal relationships, social transaction, learning, and recreation.

When I observe our culture's treatment of those who suffer mental illness, I have alternating feelings of shame and anger. I am ashamed of a culture where people are discarded and neglected like trash, where helpless human beings are routinely discharged into a hostile community. And I am angry that this culture makes weapons defense, big-business interests, and opulence its priorities, while allowing its mental health system to be powered by a minimalism of care. Mental health programs are, in my experience, understaffed and underfunded, and mental health workers—for the most part, dedicated and caring human beings—are swamped with caseloads that diminish time for individualized support. It is madness within madness.

In my personal relationships with the mentally ill, some of whom have become close friends of mine over twenty-five years on the streets, I try to compensate for this lack of care. I relate differently to each mentally ill person I encounter, tailoring my approach based on the circumstances of each. I am more careful, more delicate when I talk with them, because one does not know what is happening inside the brain of a mentally ill person. The more articulate of them will tell me that. They are, first of all, God's creatures, and therefore they deserve the love and awe intrinsic to all creatures. And second of all, they deserve the best kind of spiritual and psychological assistance available.

Guided by these two ideas, I become what I can be for them. I am a good and steady listener; a friend; a father; an interested, yet not patronizing, party; a compassionate priest; a truth teller; a companion they can rely on to walk with them through the darkness; and a trusted individual who will make the case for them in their fight for professional mental health care.

Of course there are risks: some will put the face of a demon on me, some will threaten me with harm, some will walk away from me because personal connection is too painful, some will laugh at me as if I belong to a race of sappy clowns, some will develop crushes and come on to me, some will become obsessive about seeing me.

It is worth the risks. Nothing is as wonderful as knowing that people who have been rejected by society for their entire life can find a moment of peace and happiness in the presence of someone who legitimately cares for them and has no other agenda but being with them. Maybe it will be a window to life that no one had quite taken the time to help them open. I have known such moments.

■ ■ ■

I recently met a wonderful man, Rodney. He lives in one of the hotels. He is a short and stocky man, friendly, and the owner of an irresistible cackling laugh. He suffers from a mild form of schizophrenia, which drives his extraordinary imagination. He moves in his fantasy world of time travel, witches, wars, and goblins with a kind of casual, unaffected arrogance, talking about it as one would talk about his or her superior athletic prowess or unlimited professional contacts.

We met in the lobby of his hotel at a birthday party sponsored by the Macdonald Center, which throws parties once a month for residents who are celebrating birthdays.

A day after our first meeting, as I was walking to an appointment, Rodney chased me down in order to pass on some breathtaking information about the enemy. He assured me that I was a leader and that I would be protected "when the Russians land in Portland," an arrival that was imminent, according to his sources. Furthermore, should anyone give me trouble, he said, furtively looking over his shoulder, they would be dealt with. He went on to tell me that troublemakers would be brought to his submarine, located at the bottom of the Indian Ocean, where they would be interrogated and then strapped to an armed torpedo and sent into the unforgiving depths.

What is scary about talking with Rodney, from my point of view, is that I can get into his conspiracy fantasies. I go with his flow, not in a condescending or patronizing manner but in the way a friend shares a game with a friend. There is always a gleam in his eyes when he is revealing his furiously serious observations about life.

One day, while gabbing with Rodney on the street, I mentioned that there were a couple of local politicians who bugged me and maybe deserved the torpedo tour. I chuckled to myself at how clever I was.

Rodney stopped walking, paused, looked at me with sadness, and said, "You know, Father Gary, sometimes you sound a bit crazy."

■ ■ ■

I had pizza with Charles yesterday. Periodically we do this, chatting over beers (which he buys) and food (which I buy) in a little pizza joint not far from my place and his SRO hotel. He was slurring a bit, which I attributed to his medication. He is a wonderful individual, a forty year old who lives with schizophrenia, which he keeps at bay with proper medication. He never knew his real parents, but he was raised by some decent foster parents. As he ate his pizza, he rambled on about many important things, from his group therapy to his young daughter, whom he hadn't seen since she was four months old.

This particular night, he was also bummed out by the fact that his cat had died, finished off by a mouse that was in the process of being finished off by some D-Con poison. It was heartrending to hear him talk of the cat as someone with whom he could "communicate" in a building full of people who did not talk to one another. He added that the cat sort of took the place of "all those people who never come to see me or take time to talk with me."

Oh, the ache we have to know and be known, to love and be loved.

■ ■ ■

Jody returned to the streets recently, released (prematurely, I think) by the mental health system. She has aged, and she rants and raves more than ever. She talks in a perpetual whine, a whine that is born of her mentally ill perception that the world is out to unfairly punish her.

No shelter will take her because of past disruptions. Even if she had money, most of the Burnside hotels would not want her. She needs to take her medication but will not do so. Without her medication she is a sitting duck for the attacks of her mental illness. A street person once told me, "She has a big mouth, Father, and someone is going to whack her," so I am forever afraid that someone will hit her because of her inappropriate words. Or I fear she will decide "No one will help me, so I give up" and drift into a catatonic state.

Jerome, a Macdonald Center staff person, recently described to me an incident of Jody's acting-out anger. Apparently he had told her that if she didn't stop a certain kind of behavior she would be escorted off the premises. Her face chiseled with fury, she looked at him sternly and proceeded to urinate on the chair in which she was seated. I thought at the time that her attitude gave new meaning to the expression "Piss on you."

She was unreachable, trapped on that vicious merry-go-round of mental illness: sickness, bizarre behavior, institutionalization, medication, stability, release, abandonment of medication regimen, sickness.

And the ride goes on.

■ ■ ■

Noel was a cheerful man with a classic dual diagnosis: mental illness and drug addiction. His drug use would come and go, but he was always careful not to be around me when he was stoned. He used to see me at a distance down a city street and call out my name, and once he knew I had spotted him, he would unleash peals of laughter, like someone who threw you a surprise party and caught you unawares as you walked through the door. Anyone who worked at the chapel or at the Macdonald Center received the same audacious treatment.

Short and stocky, with raccoon shadows under dark eyes that gleamed when he laughed, he was both my biggest fan and my Spanish teacher. He was Nicaraguan by birth and escaped from that country during the Somoza regime. I helped him manage his money, which was difficult sometimes, because in addition to the subsidy he received for his mental illness, he earned money by putting his bilingualism to use. Since I never saw that extra money, it was hard to tell how much he was spending beyond his subsidy. At one time in his life he wanted to be in a religious order, but his mental health prevented it; nevertheless, his prayer life was rich and edifying. I think some of his happiest moments were the days he spent at a local monastery.

Noel was a soft touch, which meant two things: first, he would care for hurting people who were on the streets and would buy them food; and second, he would be taken advantage of by predators who sensed his naiveté and desire to be liked. Noel saw everyone as a potential friend.

Periodically Noel would mix up his psychotropic medications or lose track of his schedule for taking them and wind up in the hospital or in a state of confusion. One such incident stands out. It happened the day after he was sworn in as a U.S. citizen at the federal building. He walked into the chapel that night, looking for me. He was wearing the same sports coat, shirt, and tie he wore to his swearing-in ceremony, but nothing else besides a pair of boxer shorts. I was sure it was a screwup in his medication and probably a little cocaine. He informed me with a dazed smile that he was ready to go to the swearing-in ceremony. Disorientation *totalmente*. How strange we must have looked to anyone driving by Burnside and Broadway at 10 P.M. that night ("Honey, check out the little fellow with no pants hanging on to the big gray-haired guy"). Of course, Noel, blissfully out of it, was chattering away as if we were in the middle of our Spanish conversation class.

One Tuesday Noel missed our morning appointment. On reflection I realized I had not seen him all weekend, and I became worried and anxious. My hunch was that he was in trouble or worse, so I went to his hotel and the hotel manager and I checked his apartment.

The first thing that hit us—like a fist—was the smell of Noel's decomposing body. He was lying between his bed and the wall, where he had probably lain dead since Friday night. There was drug paraphernalia on the floor, in the kitchenette, in the bathroom. A little part of me died in that room.

I called his brother in California and then his sister, whom I had visited in San Salvador two years earlier. Then I just wept and walked, walked and wept. I was numb, discouraged, and feeling some lurking guilt about not having done more, been more perceptive. I spent part of that night on the phone, talking with those here who knew and loved Noel and with distant friends who, though they never met him, knew him on my face and in my voice.

Occasionally in life one meets an individual who leaves an indelible imprint on the soul. Noel was such a person for me. He touched me with his holiness, for I always felt stronger and more in touch with life when Noel told me that he was praying for me. And I will always remember his laughter, whether it was ringing down a street out of the sheer joy of seeing me or in my room as I butchered another Spanish idiom. It used to intoxicate me, that laughter, like the embrace of someone I loved, calling forth a wonderful part of my heart to be claimed.

A few days after Noel's death, his older brother, Carlos, arrived at the airport, a dead ringer for Noel, with a few more gray hairs. We picked up the cremated remains and then went to Noel's room, where Carlos selected a few religious articles that he knew the family would want. Before I took him to his plane on the same day, we prayed over the ashes in my room at the chapel. I read from the book of Wisdom in Spanish, a favorite of Noel's. Carlos and I cried some more.

Carlos had a singular dignity about him. He was a consummate family man, and though he was aware of Noel's problems and history, he never wavered in his understanding, love, and care for his brother, Noelito. He took the ashes to be buried next to the graves of their parents in the little Nicaraguan coastal town where Noel had grown up.

Que Dios te bendiga, Noelito.

■ ■ ■

One of the challenges and heartaches for all of us who live and work in Old Town is maintaining a relationship with a difficult person. Every staff person who works in mental health, or in counseling, or in social work, or in shelters, or in drop-in centers, or in soup kitchens knows the feeling: you want to assist someone, but that person is a total turnoff. It is as though the person is plotting to alienate you. And yet, in most cases, especially with the mentally ill or with someone who was severely psychologically damaged in childhood, the person does not know that his or her behavior is obnoxious.

Lucy is a case in point. She is a young, mentally ill, developmentally disabled woman. She is obese, unattractive, and dirty most of the time. She lives in a trashed apartment full of cartloads of junk she has harvested from the streets. Her obsessive-compulsive disorder renders her unable to pass up anything.

Her room is a cave of chaos and filth, yet she rejects any criticism of her lifestyle or suggestions for change. She has a difficult time listening, and her mind seems locked on to thoughts that have nothing to do with what the person addressing her is saying; inevitably she challenges from another point of view. She will talk incessantly unless one cuts her off. It is amazing and sad. The paradox for Lucy is that each time she reaches out, she does so in such an offensive manner that human contact is impossible. She is like a rogue gene, wanting to belong yet of such a nature that the rest of the body must reject it.

And yet, for all the tearing-the-hair-out-of-my-head conversations I have had with Lucy, I inevitably sense how desperate she is for attention and help. She is a daughter of God. This is why I hang in there with her and make an effort to talk with her. I have seen her intelligence. I get the feeling that she maintains her torrent of anecdotal commentary about the dirty deals she is getting in order to keep me around her. I have never lost sight of the hard truth that she has grown up unloved, unwanted, untouched, unengaged. Her life has been a nightmare of survival.

And yet, is she not one of the least of the sisters and brothers to whom Jesus refers? In a culture that deifies physical beauty, she lives in a constant storm of unattractiveness. Isn't the flip side of all her attention-seeking a desperate plea for friendship, love, care, attention, meaning? I often hear people categorize the poor mentally ill as individuals who "should know better and could improve if they tried." Such judgments, made about a person such as Lucy, are the sanctimonious judgments of fools.

■ ■ ■

Rodney was at church the other day, wearing some stylish black sunglasses and a hooded sweatshirt, the hood pulled over his head. After Mass he informed me that he had given up on being a witch and was now a monk. I asked him if he was associated with any particular group of monks. He took off his glasses, looked at me as if he was about to give me some top-secret information, and said that the whole world would soon know, but he could tell me: his order comes from a very distant star system that is directly in line with the island of Zanzibar.

Replacing his glasses, Rodney the monk, comfortable resident alien and enigmatic mystic and former witch, wished me good evening and slid into the night, deep in thought, his mysterious cowl pulled over his head.

■ ■ ■

While waiting for the 6:00 transporter bus to the Portland Airport the other morning, whom should I see stroll up but Dan, the former ordained minister. His mental illness takes him on ups and downs, more downs than ups. He is able to function on the streets, though his condition is severe enough that he can receive Supplemental Security Income. He is usually scruffy in appearance, mercurial, dreadfully serious, and defensive. When he talks, he demonstrates both quick intelligence and aggressiveness. He loves to talk theology with me and hates to discuss psychology. The latter subject, if brought up, shifts him into attack mode.

I was not in the mood for conversation, but I girded my loins for his blitzkrieg of opinion about whatever was on his mind. Noting that I had my suitcase, he smirked and made some crack like "Oh, I see you are leaving us. Whatsamatter, don't have time for the poor anymore?"

I asked him why he was so angry. Wrong question. He spent the next ten minutes lambasting me for being "Mr. Psychologist" and for being indifferent toward the homeless and the issues of the homeless. It was clear to him that I was a priest in the inner city for the sole purpose of pimping the poor, hiding behind my middle-class education and my mighty Jesuit graduate degrees.

I think I have learned over the years how to finesse the madness of the streets in all its many-headed forms. I rode him out, knowing that deep down he was hurting and saw in me something that he was not able to be anymore. Essentially he liked me. I told him that I only had a few minutes before my bus arrived, that I did not mean to offend him, and that I was preoccupied about a meeting to which I was going and for which, as usual, I was not prepared.

He pondered it all, apparently decided that what I had said was legitimate, and calmed down. Offering me a cigarette, he said, "Yeah, well, I can get pretty snotty sometimes. By the way, Gary, have you read any good theology books lately?"

I told him of essays I had been reading by Karl Rahner, the deceased German heavy, whom I knew to be one of his favorite theo-logians. As my bus arrived, he gave me two bucks "for some coffee at the airport to clear your head before that damn meeting."

What happened? How did this guy wind up on the streets? And what, in providence, am I to be for him? An island of predawn meaning in a life that is tormented and disconnected? I think so. I know he longed to make contact with a brother, no matter how twisted the corridors were that led to that touch.

■ ■ ■

Mental illness that has a religious dimension can have many manifestations. It can result in paranoia and the conviction that the end of time is lying under every rock. Often it inspires delusions of grandeur, leading one to think that he or she is Jesus or Buddha or God almighty. I have encountered individuals who have introduced themselves as a handpicked lieutenant of all the above. Those who maintain such a belief either exhibit pious condescension toward the uninitiated or wave a warning finger in your face, the way Mom used to do, a sort of "you better get with it, young man" approach. Sometimes this belief can be accompanied by voices from the other side, offering one revelation after another and telling the subject of the way things are from moment to moment.

■ ■ ■

Joanie, a woman in her twenties, frail and lovely, carries herself like an unadorned princess. Her illness, though, can at times subject her to disorientation and great suffering. She is plagued by voices that hammer away at her good heart, rebuking her around the clock for her unspeakable, unredeemable sins.

Not on her medication, she came to me the other day and spoke the language of those condemning voices; at such moments, the inner demons are at full strength. It is fragile territory for a priest. It is important for me to speak to her about taking advantage of all the means available to her, like her medication and her counseling, and about the fact that God did not make her evil.

For the most part, Joanie is positive in her faith, and she is also wonderfully open about it. She was recently spotted reading Scripture to a mounted policeman while his partner was busting someone. Knowing her loving ways, I'm sure she was just trying to bring a moment of consolation and peace to a stressful job. I must ask her what Scripture passages she uses for Portland's finest.

Not long ago she wrote up a petition for the city council, requesting that they do a better job of cleaning up Old Town. She closed the document with "in the name of Jesus Christ. Amen." Ah, what I would have given to see the expressions on the faces of the council staff when these lovingly crafted petitions came in. For the most part, I think petitions are a waste of time. But I signed this one.

One day I escorted a mutual friend of ours to the courthouse to deal with a misdemeanor charge: trespassing. Joanie came along to comfort him. He had been ticketed for urinating in a vacant parking lot. It sounded more like police harassment to me. He had spent the last two weeks worrying himself to a frazzle over every possible outcome short of the rack. This, of course, is because he has already spent more than half of his fifty years incarcerated, most of it in the state penitentiary.

In the end, he was informed that no complaint had been filed, so the whole thing was dropped. We started to leave the courtroom quickly, because I didn't want the court to change its mind. But there was Joanie, turning and saying to a stunned judge and the assembled legions, "God bless you."

So much for the separation of church and state. I cringed as I pushed the two of them ahead of me, expecting the judge to say, "Now wait a minute, you three, come back here, especially that gray-haired guy."

Who is most in touch with religious reality: Joanie or me? Notwithstanding her periodic bouts with negative religious thoughts, she has an amazing childlike wisdom when she talks about God. It is in such moments that I lose track of what is mental illness and what is the power of the Spirit working through a person. I have found that the spirit of piety in the mentally ill is stronger and more devotional and more other-oriented than that of much of formal religious life. Maybe that is part of the point: Joanie is to teach me.

■ ■ ■

In a conversation with Jerome, a staff person at the Macdonald Center, Rodney pointed out that Jesus Christ at one time lived in West Virginia under the name of Edgar Allen Poe.

"Well, Rodney," asked Jerome, "where is he now and what name is he using?"

There followed a silent and disbelieving look from Rodney. And then he said to Jerome: "You don't know who he is? *You don't know who he is?*"

"Uh-uh," responded Jerome.

Rodney slowly surveyed the room, ensuring that all present were safe and could be trusted with the forthcoming truth, and then, with Moses-like inspiration and conviction, he exclaimed to Jerome, "It's Gary Smith!"

One of the results of this latest stunning Rodney revelation is that I am now being called "J. C." by the Macdonald Center staff. Rodney, of course, does not know that *I* know who *he* thinks I really am. Which is all very funny, because sometimes I haven't a clue who I am.

■ ■ ■

I was at Theo's place today. He is a gentle, developmentally disabled man who suffers also from schizophrenia, someone I have visited in a variety of SROs over the years. Hotel managers, even the most tolerant, usually wind up having a problem with his lack of apartment care. His room is always some version of the same scenario: dirty floors, unwashed dishes, empty Spam cans, cigarette butts everywhere, false teeth on whatever is serving as a coffee table, dirty sheets. As much as his mental health workers try, they cannot convince him to clean up his digs, so he eventually gets the hook by management.

He always keeps seven tiny plastic horses on some available flat surface in his room. "They keep the ghosts away," he told me early in our acquaintance.

Theo often says things that betray a childlike perception of the world. One day, reflecting on God's goodness, he said nonchalantly: "I pray for everyone. And, Brother Gary, I pray for God, too. He needs help." He said this as though he was speaking of a needy friend who could use some backup once in a while. In his life, he works from the premise that God is a sweetheart. And he prays this way, totally accepting of this theological truth and totally available to the one he calls "Sweetheart." It is the street version of what St. Ignatius calls consolation without previous cause, when an individual is experiencing God directly without any thought, event, or person being the source of such a movement. I think Theo is in that state almost all of the time.

He lives with the fantasy that he has won the Irish Sweepstakes, but for some reason the payoff check—for hundreds of millions of dollars—has been tied up in the postal system. What is eerily wonderful about his longing to finally cash in on his lucky ticket is that he never thinks of spending a cent on himself. Although the irate SRO managers of Old Town might disagree, this man, as far as I can see, does not have a selfish bone in his body. He will periodically tell me and my visiting partner that his first expenditure will be for an enormous center for the homeless, with "special places for the women and their children because they suffer a lot more than us men." All the millions are to be spent on the poor "because the rich don't need it." Then, inevitably, he will look at the two of us and say that he will buy us a house and a car and anything else we might need. This is a man who has thought it all through.

Theo and I were chatting one day on a park bench when a disheveled man, mumbling to himself, shuffled by. Theo tried to get his attention but failed. The man was in his own inner world and did not see either one of us. Theo said, "I wanted to give him some money. A dollar or two. I like to help people on the road; I was on the road once and people helped me."

On leaving, I grasped his hand and told him that I would be praying for him. "Well, now, isn't that a beautiful thought," he said. "Yessir, that sure is a beautiful thought. And I'll pray for you, too, Brother Gary. Yessir, I sure will."

As I was walking to my residence, I thought of his last remark. *A beautiful thought.* A beautiful thought. When I think of him, it is a beautiful thought. Theo teaches me about being myself, and he touches the deepest part of my heart. How can it be otherwise? With Theo, I am in the presence of one who has no agenda, who transparently cares for me and could give a shit about any of the things that are supposed to impress people. He takes me purely as I am, which allows me to be who I am. That is the way we all want to be before the sweet heart of God.

■ ■ ■

The best time for Norman and me to talk was over a pizza and a beer. As we were gabbing, I described to him a poor guy I had seen the night before, who seemed to be having an argument with an Old Town trash can. One of my reflections was that it was impossible to understand what was going through the mind of that man, ranting on and on and challenging the unresponsive container to a fight.

Norman listened carefully. Now in his late thirties, he had endured the slings and arrows of schizophrenia since he was a teenager. He studied me for a second and then said that he knew exactly how that person felt, because he himself was there once and is never far away from the mental disintegration and dysfunction that I had witnessed the previous evening.

Norman is a slender man, very intelligent, personable, and caring. He is capable of some bone-crushing hugs in which he affirms how much he loves me. He can also experience sudden tidal waves of anger. I have seen him stomp out of my office, yelling and screaming, huffing and puffing, hurling curses upon the building and all of its inhabitants. Yet, invariably, he is back in half an hour, tail between his legs, apologizing. The furious whiteout has passed.

The more we know the object of our love, the more we love that object. That is the way I feel about Norman. A large part of this love is based on his honesty. Norman is disarmingly honest about his life. He once described to me his long stay in a mental hospital, where he was sent because he was a menace to himself and others. Over time, as his mental state stabilized and improved, he asked to be given a less isolated living situation and better opportunity for therapy, especially in group settings. He felt that he needed to go to the next level if he was going to grow. It was during one of our pizza sessions that he explained this need in terms of the horseshoe analogy.

"During my teenage years," Norman said, "I was in a horseshoe-throwing league. Like any competition, teams were pitted against teams that had a similar skill level. My experience was that the better the competition, the better I did. You need good horseshoe players around you to improve your own skills. I felt that way in the mental hospital and vaguely realized it when I was sleeping under bridges and mumbling to myself on the streets like your friend talking to the trash container. If they kept me doped up all day like a zombie, there was no way I was going to improve. I needed people involved in my daily life who might be able—through their own kind of experience—to help me grow. The mental institution staff got the message and accommodated me. I moved up to another group of horseshoe throwers. Eventually, I was given the opportunity to make it on the outside."

And so he has. With proper medication, regular counseling sessions, and a sustaining family like Outreach Ministry or the Macdonald Center, Norman is able to live a decent life. He will always have to deal with his disability and live as a poor man because he cannot hold down a steady job, but he will be able to live his life without the fragmentation caused by a disease that once ruled his life.

Not all can do it.

■ ■ ■

I had a sad encounter today with Darnell. He has suffered from schizophrenia since his sophomore year in college, and the illness ended his promising college career. He also has a substance abuse problem. Between the booze and the illness, he has become more and more of a problem for his present payees, his parents. Since the onset of his illness, his parents have steadily become the object of his negative acting out.

His parents had decided that they couldn't be his payees anymore, so he was interviewing with OMB. His father, a professor at a local university, was present for the interview. Naturally, Darnell was suspicious of me and declared to his father that he did not want help.

I told him, "You don't have any choice, Darnell. The government office that provides a subsidy for you [Supplemental Security

Income] has determined that you cannot handle your own money, and therefore you need a payee, and your parents have decided to switch the payees."

That said, Darnell laid in to me and his father, blaming us for everything that was haywire in his universe.

His is not a happy prognosis, as any psychologist or recovering alcoholic will tell me. Unlike many of the schizophrenics who wander the streets of America, Darnell will survive, if for no other reason than that he has a good and intelligent family who, despite their pain, will advocate for him.

His parents are broken and bewildered by their son's illness. I can see it in the father's eyes. Even their well-developed coping strategies have begun to break down, because no matter how good their efforts to love him are, the sickness is always able to outgun them. After his hospitalization, Darnell wound up coming home, only to revert to his old ways.

How many nights of uncertainty? How much pain over a child who has disappeared but still sleeps in your house? How much guilt over the anger at so much apparently useless time invested?

Darnell did not like outreach. The issue is institutional control. It is a mentally ill person's catch-22. He must get financial assistance to survive, to ensure some freedom, but the only way he can do it is to have a money manager and, therefore, from his perspective, no freedom. When one is mentally ill, there are obstacles everywhere.

■ ■ ■

Today I led a memorial service for Al in the lobby of the Foster Hotel. He was a man who had affected many people.

Clyde showed up and asked to sing a song in memory of Al. For some reason, Clyde has been singing a lot lately. Al was his buddy, and so out of respect for their friendship he wanted to sing "Amazing Grace," a regular in Clyde's repertoire. He sang, and we were all appreciative.

Many people in the room made poignant comments about Al. From the back of the room, Darlene, gaunt, thin, weeping gently, burned out by alcohol, related that "Al was the only guy who ever spoke to me."

Rodney, shifting into his fantasy life, talked about a conversation he had had with Al that concerned their mutual war experiences. Rodney, of course, has been fighting wars relentlessly since the American Revolution. Turns out that he and Al both fought in the Civil War.

"But do you want to hear something amazing?" Rodney innocently asked. He paused dramatically. "We were both prisoners in that war, but on *opposite* sides of the conflict!"

■ ■ ■

Frank stopped me on the streets as I was running to beat the rain. Could we talk? Sure, I told him. We ducked into a coffee shop.

We hadn't spoken in a while, but our friendship went back to my first days in Portland. Frank is a relatively young man, overweight, with huge sad eyes that always have a pleading look, as if he desperately hopes the world will forgive him. He is gentle and good.

Sighing and taking a long drag on his cigarette, he said, "I saw you walking across the street, Father, and felt like I needed to talk to you."

He proceeded to describe his pain, a result of his illness, paranoid schizophrenia, and the hard life he has lived. His struggles were centered on his fear that the police were out to charge him with murder (from his perspective, narcs and cops were everywhere, watching him). In addition, there were voices coming through the walls of his room, and people were making derogatory remarks about his religion.

"People call me a fag and all that and, well, you know, Father."

I didn't know, but I tried to be present to him. I knew he was seeing me because I was a priest and not a psychiatrist, so I tried to offer some nonpsychological help. Nevertheless, I tried to determine during our talk and ensuing talks whether he was seeing his mental health counselor on a regular basis. He was. Before we went our separate ways, I asked him if he would like to pray together. Yes, he would. It brought a measure of peace to his weary face.

One day Frank showed up at my OMB office, frantic. He was hounded and haunted by delusions of paranoia, which he spoke of through tears of confusion. It was a story that I have heard before (he does not remember that he told me), but with some new sinister details: CIA hunters and watchers, mind-control technology that CIA agents have acquired from space aliens, and a voice of condemnation that constantly tells him, "You are evil, you are weak, you will be punished." His was the personal agony of the paranoid who has crossed over from reality to the compelling demands of his mind.

To Frank, the minions of the CIA are everywhere. We went to a coffee shop to talk, and at one point in our conversation, Frank pointed with his eyes and an almost imperceptible movement of his hand at the person sitting at the next table. He mouthed silently, warning me, "Seeee Eye Aiiii." When they were not watching him talk with me, they were operating a mind-control machine in his hotel. There are fiber-optic cameras everywhere; no one can be trusted.

We grabbed our coffee and left and finished off the coffee walk with a prayer and my editorial comment that I don't care who is watching me just so I know that God is watching me, too. Frank said that this was a very important thought for him to carry.

What breaks my heart is to hear him talk about the severe punishment that will be administered to him. Once, he said, "My pain will include cattle prods in prison and a kind of pain that no one has suffered since Jesus. And to escape the CIA is futile. Even you, Father Gary, can't get away. And now that you know, I am sorry to say, you too may be killed."

Now, that was a statement that gave me goose bumps. It is not that I fear Frank so much as I wonder where his paranoia might drive him. Would he wake up one day and conclude that I was part of the conspiratorial plot to get him, an agent of the devil masquerading as a priest (a "man of God," as he liked to call me)?

I'll take my chances. I like him very much.

On another occasion, shortly after Christmas, Frank came to me looking as though he hadn't slept in weeks. He was experiencing a lot of delusions about mutilations, and government agents were involved in the whole mess. At that point I felt more than ever his loneliness. So I lingered with him for a long time, and we went down by the Willamette River to look at some of the Christmas lights. He relaxed.

On the way back he said an interesting and humbling thing. "It gives me strength to see you walking down here in Old Town. You care, Father; people don't care, but you do. It is inspiring to see you, and that is why I came over to see you, to talk with you and to pray."

I thanked him for his trust, and we prayed as we walked back to his hotel. He left me, a hint of a smile on his face. He was like someone who had stumbled into a quiet little creek after a day of tough mountain climbing.

I thought later that Frank's hunt is for the affirmation of movements inside of him that are constantly struggling to assert themselves: love, meaning, truth, and the notion that God is stronger than the voices that assail him. I believe his search is guided by the heart of God expressing a longing for Frank and for his wholeness. I don't want that to sound naive. I know there is no quick religious fix for mental illness short of a miracle. I know, too, that mental illness can propel the religious instinct into the worst kind of madness. But my experience with the mentally ill on the streets is that there is a place in them that is sacred, and they can touch it in the presence of one whom they can trust, a person committed to walking with them through the minefields. I believe that the heart of God is enfleshed in the depths of friendship with another human being, whether it be with a person I love or with my coffee buddy, Frank.

It is in this premise that a Jesuit priest like me, riddled with warts and weaknesses, discovers the purpose of his hands and heart. I am a small sign of the church bearing Christ to the world.

It is in the presence of Frank that I am drawn out of myself and set off down the path that will lead me to the wounded and along which I will find my life and holiness. Frank teaches me the way to the fundamental task of the church, which is to tell the poor of this world that God loves them.

chapter four

WHAT ARE YOU INTO?:

THE SEARCH FOR INDIGNATION

Out of the rubble of my life—so undeserving,
insignificant, obscure, and screwed up—
Jesus crafts someone who will, in spite of himself,
bear fruit for the kingdom and the glory of God.
It never ceases to amaze me.

Five Jesuit novices were downtown recently, checking out agencies where they could spend part of their week working among the poor, a life-giving complement to the long haul of Jesuit studies. Man, they seemed young. But I am always happy to see them, because they should be here. Being with the poor, loving the poor, and becoming poor are among the pillars upon which a Jesuit must build his life. Whatever we become in terms of future work, whatever positions of power we hold, whatever cocktail parties we might attend, whatever shoulders we may rub, our lives must be rooted in the passion for the poor that Christ had. There we will find ourselves.

In reflecting tonight on the novices and the Jesuits, I remembered the lines penned by former President John Adams to former President Thomas Jefferson in 1816 upon learning that the Society of Jesus, once suppressed, was gathering again: "If ever there was a body of men who merited eternal damnation on earth and in hell, it is this Society of Loyola's."

I love those lines. It's one extreme view.

Here's mine.

In 1977, I was passing though New York City's JFK Airport on my way to the West Coast. I had about three hours before my connecting flight to San Francisco, so I was sitting in an airport bar having a cold beer. I was tired and really did not want to be bothered; I just wanted peace and quiet. That's when the Traveler from Hell took the seat next to mine. He began with a cheery "Hi" and intrusive icebreaker questions to which I mumbled some answers. Not discouraged, he drove deeper into my territory.

"So, what are you into?"

I made a comment about my trip. He really didn't care.

"Want to know what I'm into?"

"What?" I responded.

He said—I swear it—"I'm into darts."

Turns out that darts is a big sport in Scotland, where he had just visited. He finished me off with "Want to see my darts?"

My introvert persona went into total warp drive. I looked at this guy's silver darts briefly and then headed for another bar.

But I thought about his question at its most fundamental level: What are Jesuits into?

INTO JESUS

Well, it starts with Jesus and the words of John's Gospel: "You did not choose me, no, I chose you . . . to go out and to bear fruit, fruit that will last" (John 15:16).

First of all and last of all and most of all, we are into a relationship with Jesus. It is a relationship that changes our lives. His dreams and passions have become ours. He makes sense of our life and our commitments in a world that thinks what we are doing is naiveté at best and folly at worst. He has turned our world upside down.

So we believe that it is better to be generous than selfish, better to be true than false, better to be a brave person than a coward, better to be compassionate than self-absorbed, better to embrace peace than violence, better to be just than unjust, better to love without cost than to play life safe, better to walk our talk than to whine from the sidelines, better to have nothing than to have everything, better to be chaste and poor and obedient than to cruise through life committed to no ideal, no dream, no person.

That same relationship has put me in spots I never dreamed possible: with people who ignored me or hated me, with people who resented some arrogant and sanctimonious Jesuit telling them anything, with individuals who cried out for authenticity and had nothing to give me but the purity of their hearts, with a precious few who fell in love with me and I with them.

Christ's mysterious union with me has given me an indelible understanding of what Dorothy Day said about her encounter with God: "I always had a sense of being followed, of being desired, a sense of hope and expectation."

In the midst of all this, I have experienced, time and time again, the absurdity of my being chosen. Out of the rubble of my life—so undeserving, insignificant, obscure, and screwed up—Jesus crafts someone who will, in spite of himself, bear fruit for the kingdom and the glory of God. It never ceases to amaze me.

That relationship with Jesus drives Jesuits toward others. Just as surely as the Holy Spirit impelled Jesus to move out toward the Jordan and beyond, the heart of Christ drives us into human hearts. And branded on our hearts are the poor.

INTO THE POOR

> *The spirit of the Lord Yahweh has been given to me,*
> *for Yahweh has anointed me.*
> *He has sent me to bring good news to the poor,*
> *to bind up hearts that are broken.*
>
> ISAIAH 61:1

Jesuits, because they are into a relationship with Jesus, are into a relationship with the poor. If anything is a reflection of the beauty of the life that a Jesuit chooses, it is our desire to be with, and to bring the good news of God's heart to, the poor, the abandoned, the despised, and all those shorn of dignity.

When I think of this, I always turn my heart and mind toward the memory of six Salvadoran brother Jesuits who were gunned down in 1989 along with their housekeeper and her daughter. They were killed because they were into the poor: organizing the poor, speaking for the poor, angry for the poor. In 1995, I was in the garden where they were executed by Salvadoran soldiers. Kneeling there, I thought: *Here people were killed because they dared to think and write and research and act in the name of the heart of Christ and therefore opposed the oppression that was denying humanity to the majority of the people of El Salvador.* In a word, they sought to change structures that crush people. It was their way of proclaiming the good news of God's love, of binding up the hearts of the broken. And they were murdered for it.

Jesuit Jon Sobrino was a housemate of the six slain Jesuits but was in Thailand when the murders took place. He wrote: "A poor Church is, by its very nature, more compassionate, and a compassionate Church is, by its very nature, poorer."

Among the poor, we learn to internalize their suffering, and we are transformed into the heart of Christ. We adopt a viewpoint that forever passionately directs our behavior. Sobrino said: "Our compassion is a very specific form of love: love in practice, which arises when one is confronted with the unjustly inflicted suffering of others and acts to eliminate it for no other motive than the very existence of that suffering—and without being able to offer any excuse for not doing so."

The poor teach us to be truth tellers: to speak to what must be done to transform oppressive structures even as we are meeting individual needs. The poor teach us of compassion: to feel another's heartache even as we are creating concrete practices of relief. The poor teach us to embark on the sacred search for indignation: to discover our anger in the face of the greed, malice, and human indifference that give birth to suffering and to speak to it. No, we must yell about it. As Salvadoran archbishop Oscar Romero rebuked his government: "If you strike my people, you strike me."

In our culture of wealth there are people who do not have proper diets, health care, education, or housing simply because they are poor. Period. I live in an area where sumptuous condos exist within shouting distance of people standing in line for a cheese sandwich. This is the stuff of indignation.

Ignatius wanted Jesuits to be poor and be with the poor. Not because he wanted a bunch of good guys, not because he didn't want us to work with the wealthy—in fact, Ignatius spent lots of time with the wealthy—but because he knew that the poor could break us open and teach us how to be who we really are called to be: people who seek to know, love, and serve Jesus Christ.

INTO COMPANIONSHIP

Finally, I would say to my dart-throwing friend and to any Jesuit novice who happens along on the streets and in the SROs of Portland, Jesuits are into companionship with other Jesuits. God has placed us with other individuals who will be, in providence, the ones in and around whom we will be in service, in and around whom we have fallen in love with Christ.

One night, when I was in Toronto undergoing my studies and having a very difficult time, I returned to my room to find two beers sitting on my desk. Shortly afterward, a Jesuit from Detroit came in and said, "It looks like you need to talk, so I thought we could do it over a brew."

Indeed. It was a wonderful reaching out of a brother Jesuit. I think now of that moment and remember the line from the book of Proverbs: "Brother helped by brother is a fortress" (Proverbs 18:19). That moment, such an authentic one, has never left me. It is a norm against which I can measure the love and care I give and experience in my ministry with the Jesuits.

I have known many Jesuits over the years, from several countries and of all ages. Some of us are self-absorbed jerks, and some of us are class acts; some of us are crabby and cantankerous, and some of us are tender and personable; some are stuffy and obnoxious conservatives, and some crazed and obnoxious liberals; some are wounded—physically and psychologically—and some seemingly have it all together; some will be indifferent, and some will openly cherish me; some are saints, and all of us are sinners.

In this least Society of Jesus, the heart of God has destined that we discover ourselves, even as we help others to find themselves. The common bond among Jesuits is that we are all into Jesus. We've all been taken by the call of Christ the king; we all want to carry his torch into the city of darkness. He is the steel band of truth that lashes us all together.

So what are we into? Jesus, the poor, the brothers and sisters who surround us. In all of this, I have moments of howling success—when I have been so grateful that my heart aches—and moments of dreaded darkness, when my heart weeps.

Jeremiah makes it clear to me that no one chooses to fall into the hands of the living God. I am chosen. Sometimes I resist and resort to rage and bitterness, but finally I succumb—in love—to the God who has given me my identity in the first place. Such love explains why I am here and why all the people I write about in this book are so precious to me.

chapter five

CRASHING AND BURNING:

THE INSANITY OF DRUGS AND

ALCOHOL

When this disease claims a victim, there are few
human bankruptcies that can match it. But I always
have hope, and I believe that the power of God is
greater than our own helplessness and stupidity.

Bonnie's face has a million miles
worn into it, each leathery line a story. We talked one day in a
large, dreary hotel lobby, her hair hanging down in a gray mass and
her eyes peeking out at me. Sad eyes. How old is she? Forty? Fifty?
Seventy? She was sober this particular afternoon and spoke with
candor about her life. There is the vague background: the education at a northern California college, the marriage to a high-
powered lawyer, things happening, the crash and burn brought on
by heartache and booze, a string of burned-out relationships. Now
she is here, in this shitty hotel. At one point she sighed, ran her

hand through her hair, and summed it up by saying, "Father, I've been down to the corner a few times."

Yep, you have, Bonnie. Yet in spite of it all, she is a warm, intelligent, and personable woman with a great heart. One always has to adapt to Bonnie's discourse, because it seems incredible that out of that pathetically thin body, so ravaged by alcoholism, could come anything but survival language, bitter language. And yet her speech betrays dignity and no self-absorption. How, with all that she has endured—self-inflicted and inflicted by others—can she speak with such directness and self-possession? She is like a lily emerging from the mud.

She hesitated in her story, got teary eyed. What happened, Bonnie? Did the booze lead to the heartbreak, or did the heartbreak lead to the booze? Or are reasons and explanations and origins now the stuff of another planet, long lost in the journey of chaos and darkness? How did you wind up in this stinking SRO in a room stuffed with forty-ounce bottles of beer, the air saturated with unventilated cigarette smoke and the pungent smell of urine? How did you manage to hang on to your island of self-possession?

■ ■ ■

I spoke recently with a handsome and tall young man, Otis, about possible client status at Outreach Ministry. He is twenty-nine. Four years ago he was lucratively immersed in the Los Angeles drug trafficking scene when some bigger fish came along.

Otis was attacked by his rivals in the restroom of a dance hall. They broke his jaw in such a way that it cut off blood to his brain. He suffered a stroke that left him paralyzed on his right side and aphasic. He is now unable to say what he wants to say: his brain knows the words, but he can't figure out how to say them. So he uses bunches of words, hoping that the right one will come out— like casting a large net to catch a few fish. Most of the time, if I have the context, I can figure out what he is trying to say.

Here is the pathetic clincher: after all this, Otis is still using drugs. I have met other young stroke victims, their strokes induced by drugs. And yet they continue to use. It is in such a moment, when I see someone ready to inject drugs into his or her body even when that body is debilitated, that I realize the power and size and madness of drug addiction and how it will hijack one's judgment center.

I told Otis that we would not be his payee if he continued to use. OMB is not interested in supporting that kind of behavior. Otis is smart; he understood the deal and left to ponder his options.

■ ■ ■

Brenda was hanging on the corner near Burger King today. She had skipped a 2 P.M. meeting with me, and there I was, hovering over her, asking her if she still wanted to talk and could I buy her a Coke and something to eat. We talked over sandwiches and coffee. Like all stories about prostitution's path of destruction, hers was not a new one. But as always, the history that preceded the path was different.

"I am working the streets. You know that, Father. My man is in jail and will be for a long time. I lost my four kids to adoption several years ago, and after that, I just gave up. I have nothing to live for, no respect for my life. I got into crack, and after that I can't get out of this mess."

Crack. Crack cocaine. God, I hate that drug. I hate its creation; I hate the monsters who produce and deal it. I hate everything it can do to a person's head and heart. If evil had another name, it would be *crack*. The drug brings out the most selfish side of human nature. The crackhead never wants to share, never suffers compunctions of conscience. Those who have used it tell me that the only focus of the mind is on obtaining the drug. Like some hideous virus, the drug not only anesthetizes; it seizes and involves the addict. Life becomes a matter of finding the drug, preparing the drug, using it, and going on a mission to find more. Nothing can stop its voracious demands—not lovers, not mommas, not anyone or anything. Everything that is unique and beautiful about a person is submerged into darkness when he or she uses crack.

Brenda and I talked over lots of coffee; I gave her a couple of names and phone numbers of women I knew who had programs that could help her. She knew that there was no quick fix, that any choice would yield doubt and discouragement. We embraced and said good-bye.

I give her to you tonight, Lord. Use me in her life if you want.

■ ■ ■

As I was jogging yesterday morning, I saw a woman being paid off in front of a fancy hotel down on the river. I knew her, but she didn't see me. It brought to mind another prostitute, Jane, a woman I have known for years. She has a face full of heartache. Recently, when we were talking, Jane broke into tears and said, "I am so tired, Father."

As I ran on, I remembered other tired faces of women who lived by selling their bodies, often to support a drug habit, their own or that of their pimp: Dee, Tracy, Julie, Lynn . . . The list goes on, their faces as real and the sound of their voices as clear to me now as they were then, a month, a year, a decade ago. Many are dead: overdose, AIDS, murder.

I remember Gladyce, a woman I met while I was a student chaplain in a Canadian prison program that was connected to my theological studies at the University of Toronto. She was the first prostitute with whom I had ever spoken. I fell in love with her. She told me one day, in a burst of insight, that she might have a chance in life if she continued with her current course of rehab. She said that all her life she hadn't had any goals, and then she proclaimed with a hope-filled and beautiful smile, "But *I'm* a goal." On her release she called me, full of joy, and then was picked up by a former boyfriend. That same night her body was thrown from a car on a major Toronto freeway. The coroner's report indicated that she had been gang-raped and then strangled. She was twenty-three. Her death, her senseless death, crushed me for months. It has affected me to this day.

■ ■ ■

Lucia has fallen off the wagon. In seeing her slow slide back into the hell of anger, self-deprecation, and street alcoholism, I felt like I was watching the old movie *Charly*, in which the protagonist, having miraculously moved from extreme retardation to brilliance, gradually returns to a feebleminded state.

She is drinking steadily now, more and more each day. Sober, she is a woman full of exuberance and laughter, characterized by her care for the poor, her ability to talk with the poor, and that rare gift of community building. She is a shining light of grace and humanity. When she drinks, she drinks endlessly, cheap wine and beer, and hangs out with some incredible creeps. Intoxication attacks like a pack of wolves. At a crossover point she becomes vicious and mean. She manipulates me and the Outreach staff and becomes dodging, shark eyed, and selfish.

I have come to believe, having done this work for twenty years, that men outnumber women ten to one in the world of the streets. It is a dangerous world for women, full of violence that can overtake them. They have to make lots of compromises just to survive. Lucia, drinking, becomes vulnerable, and life becomes precarious.

There are those who write her off, like the cynical police officer who said, "Oh, her . . . hell, she's just a street drunk." He will never know Lucia as I have known her when she is sober and happy and creative.

Once, when I was in Fresno for a short visit, my sister, Susan, and I had dinner. Susan was in recovery at the time, had been so for more than a decade. When we got up to leave, I left about half a glass of wine on the table. She stood there, frozen for a moment, looking alternately at me and at the glass of wine. She laughed, commenting on how an alcoholic would never be able to leave any alcohol behind, unless he or she was passed out at the time. Her words spoke to the power of booze.

Susan is one of my great heroes in life, considering the conquests she has made. It is not just the matter of quitting drinking; it is all the changes one must make and the humility that one has to embrace in order to claim sobriety day in and day out.

I say all this as I ponder the collapse of Lucia. My sister gives me hope in the face of the hopelessness I feel as I watch a friend slip out of control and hand herself over to the slavery of alcohol. In the last twenty-five years, I have seen many people die prematurely either directly or indirectly because of alcoholism. When this disease claims a victim, there are few human bankruptcies that can match it. But I always have hope, and I believe that the power of God is greater than our own helplessness and stupidity.

When Lucia decides to stop drinking, I will be there to help.

■ ■ ■

I had not seen Melinda in a long time, although our friendship reached back over the years, here and in other places. She showed up at my door one night, cut loose after completing a six-week drug rehab program. Again. She needed a ride to Seattle; could I help her with a ticket? Yes, I could.

At thirty-two, she was tall and had an extraordinarily beautiful face—an exterior beauty that belied the near total self-disgust that occupied her like an invading army of parasites. At some point during the painful early years of growing up in bitter poverty and with the racist abuse of the ghetto, she had crossed over into the murky and predatory life of sex for drugs and drugs for sex. It was madness. She had a wonderful personal side, one that emerged in her honesty about her confusion and self-hate and in her longing to be happy and healthy. She had burned most of the bridges to her family and friends. But she hadn't burned the one to me.

I love this woman. True, to love her requires a certain courage and an acceptance of my tendency to make mistakes, to be excessively generous, and to be taken for a fool. Anyone who has seen addiction in operation knows this. To love her, though, does not mean I must always be prudent or that I must calculate all the pros and cons. I think love does not always look for success, nor is it blind to danger. But it does believe in the intrinsic beauty and possibility of the beloved. In the end, I believed in that sacred quality of Melinda—the presence of God—that longs for her wholeness, for the unique and living forces of her real self to develop.

There is in the world of nature constant renewal; as Gerard Manley Hopkins puts it in his poem "God's Grandeur," "There lives the dearest freshness deep down things." This renewal also takes place in our own hearts. In this renewal and in her hope for herself,

Melinda will realize her own feelings and thoughts, her wishes, interests, resources, and movements of love. This constant pull toward life is what gives her dignity. I saw this dignity in her, a dignity given to her by her Creator, independent of all the failures and bad decisions and ugly stuff that society frequently holds up as reasons for her condemnation. If I am called to anything as a priest and as a Christian, I am called to stride into—not run from—the untidiness and fear and brokenness and shame that is around me, that country of humanness in which we all live and share.

We waited briefly in the ticket line of the Greyhound station, that inner city launching pad, where people like Melinda are constantly departing toward sanity and the possibility of a new life, a life where maybe they will be able to be happy, eat with friends, and be with those who love them, a life where they may be able to freely take their children into their arms as they saunter through a city park.

One-way ticket to Seattle purchased, we had coffee and a sandwich and a cigarette together. We stood there, thinking of other streets in another place; we had been in this moment before. As her bus number was announced, she reached for me and held me close to her, weeping gently in my arms, whispering that she loved me for never giving up on her.

No, I never have. Never will.

When I think of Melinda, one movement in me is the raw gut reaction to her oppression. I hate that women like Melinda are used up sexually by pimps, made into beasts of burden by drug dealers, taunted and raped by indifferent men, beaten up by their poverty. I have known women, fearful of shelters, who spent their nights standing in storefronts, waiting until dawn, when they were safe to sleep on park benches and at bus stops; I have known women who were deliberately infected with HIV in an act of retaliation; I have known women of the streets who have been shot, stabbed, strangled, and murdered. They didn't have a chance against the power that was being used against them. You want to know about indignity inflicted on another human being? Talk to a woman of the streets.

Another movement in me is a more hushed one. It has to do with the interior beauty of women, a beauty that enables me to claim my own sensitivity and tenderness. They have taught me that the function of my chosen celibacy is not to be loveless but to contribute to the great treasure of love and sacrifice needed by humankind. The women whom I call friends—and in their midst stands dear Melinda—have uncovered me as no man could ever do and have led me into the world of loyalty and fruitfulness; they have helped me to love the mystery of myself. If a man wants to understand the heart of God, he must surely begin by standing next to the heart of a woman.

I don't have any illusions about Melinda's chances. The recidivism rate of addicts is statistically very high, as is the rate of premature deaths of addicts. So I am not kidding myself. But stats don't drive one's life of service down here. The heart does. I am not sure how God's heart connects to ours, but as I walked away from the bus depot, that connection was there, and I felt encircled by peace and joy.

> *And when he found [the lost sheep in the wilderness],*
> *would he not joyfully take it on his shoulders and*
> *then, when he got home, call together his friends and*
> *neighbors? "Rejoice with me, . . . I have found my*
> *sheep that was lost."*
>
> LUKE 15:5–7

Safe trip, Melinda.

...

Marshall tracked me down this afternoon, needing to talk. He is probably forty-five, but an old-looking forty-five, with graying hair and piercing black eyes. He's an alcoholic, worn down by the sights and emotions of his life's journey. He is alone. He rambled, clearly under the influence but feeling his story deeply. What was underneath this story? I felt his pain of going nowhere but wanting to go somewhere, like a lost child trying to find a way home.

He spoke of the people on the streets: "The people down here are children, looking always for what mommy can give them: money, a drink, cigarettes, food, a breast. They are so hungry for something no one can give them: hope."

He wobbled a bit, pondered a bench as though he was trying to see through it, and then began to cry. "I don't know what has happened to them to make them like this, something awful, painful. I wish I could help them, but I am so fucking weak, so trapped in my own body."

He spoke of past days and—like a moth that has to return to the light bulb that distracts and will eventually consume it—of the war, of his time in Southeast Asia. There was the clandestine work for the government and "the killing, the killing, the goddamn killing." "But I am a warrior," he said, trying to reassure himself.

He moved to the topic of God and said his only hope for forgiveness was Jesus. "Jesus wasn't stupid," he told me, holding my eyes. He paused. "I carried the cross on Holy Friday."

I said, "The way I read the gospel, that is what a warrior does for his king. As you said, Marshall, my man, Jesus wasn't stupid when it came to loving and forgiving. The cross is a sign of that truth."

We walked for another fifteen minutes, silently. He moved into peace.

Jesus isn't stupid. We can kid ourselves about Jesus, but he never kids himself about us. There is theology for a lifetime in that.

■ ■ ■

Occasionally I go to a Portland Rockies baseball game. The Rockies are a reasonably good minor league club. I love the intimacy of a minor league ballpark, the friendliness of the loudspeaker announcer, and all the empty-headed promotional stuff that goes on between innings. It is a long way from my headier days at the Oakland Coliseum, where I watched my beloved A's, but it is a nice evening for five bucks. It clears my head and gets my mind off the serious stuff of life.

The other night, I took a lovely woman to the ole ball game. Mary is fiftyish, has a long history of abuse by men, and is the mother of two young adults, one in college. She lives in one of the hotels in Old Town. She suffers from alcoholism, which has diminished her average intelligence but has not affected her wonderful unsophisticated excitability. Of course, though she says she loves the game, she knows virtually nothing about it, enjoying rather the ambiance of the stadium and the night probably more than can hopeless intellectuals like me, who have to figure out every managerial strategy. True to her excitable free spirit, every time Portland's mascot, Rocky Raccoon, came out, Mary would go berserk with laughter and point out to me every dumb act the raccoon performed. It became one of those situations where one goes to pieces because the other person is going to pieces. Is there anything more contagious than laughter?

Midway through the game, Mary pulled out a five-dollar bill and, with great motherly solicitude, told me to go buy myself a hot dog and beer and to please get her a diet Coke. It was one of those moments to die for. After rent, five dollars is actually a significant percentage of her monthly budget. It was the unmatchable gift that only the poor are capable of offering. I accepted it, knowing that her need to share was much more important than my sanctimonious tendency to decline.

■ ■ ■

Roe died last night in the Foster Hotel. Forty-three. His death was probably a result of his chronic alcoholism—he had a seizure that led him to choke to death on his own vomit.

He was an introvert who kept his distance from everyone, yet whom everyone liked. He was good, thoughtful, and kind. People were at ease around him. But he had this soul-wrenching pain, too, a pain that hurled him into dark cynicism and, periodically, into raging bouts of drinking. His nervous system was under attack so much from the drinking that he constantly lived under the shadow of seizures. He lived also with the inner ghost of Vietnam, which he referred to as his "psychic black hole," an experience that he would talk about only with me, and only in his most communicative days. Whatever happened in that war left him emotionally scarred. Not an uncommon story for most Nam vets. Many, like Roe, stuffed memories inside themselves. It was like burying too many corpses just below the surface of the ground; eventually all that awful poison would eat its way out. When the poison of Roe's buried memories leaked out, it led to another attack of self-destructive behavior.

He had suffered a lot physically. One night several years ago, a drunken friend of his, angry and jealous over Roe's attitude, waited for him to fall asleep, then doused him with lighter fluid and torched him. Roe's scarred shoulders and arms were a testimony to years of skin grafting.

Tomorrow morning I will have coffee with Phil, Roe's non-drinking buddy, a friend through Roe's ups and downs. Phil is the only one I know who was close to Roe, and I don't think Phil has a lot of friends either. He is devastated, of course, and bewildered by the quick end. We both learned of the death at the same time, in front of Roe's hotel. How often I saw them, especially in spring and summer mornings, walking and talking as I cruised by them on a jog. If Roe saw me, he would wave me over and then proceed to make comments about my jogging clothes, about joggers of the world, and about jogging in general—all good-humored, sarcastic zingers. He'd then dismiss me as a friend lets go of another friend with a joke.

It sounds trite to say that I'll miss him. But it is the only way to say how I feel.

■ ■ ■

Until that fateful day, I barely knew Larry, although we had occasional encounters because he was the daytime manager of one of the SROs that I visited. During those few times, he had shared with me that he was in recovery from a heroin addiction. But late one afternoon, as I was returning to the chapel, he walked up to me, his eyes very troubled. Could we talk? Of course we could talk. We slipped into an empty room at the chapel and began one of those conversations that are paradoxically frightening and deeply moving.

There had been so much pain in this man's life. He had relapsed and was now using heroin more than before. This nightmare called drug addiction is like radiation: it slashes through everything—body, soul, relationships, all that is sane and healthy and meaningful. This time the experience of slavery had brought him to a decision to end his life. Indeed, he was on the way to a bridge, where he intended to jump off. On the way to the bridge—*on the way*—he saw me coming toward him on the street. A final gasp and grab: talk to the priest.

So we talked. We wept. The guy was just beaten by it all: the helplessness, the devastation, the failure, the shame, the constant hustle for dope, the knowledge of what he had become, the sleeping under bridges, the loss of friends, the loss of the woman who once cherished him. He knew he had talents, but he also knew that he had not totally accepted his powerlessness before the addiction. It was humbling for me to be in the presence of his powerful honesty, to be part of his search for the truth.

After we talked, we prayed. I prayed to God that this man be healed, that he be clean and clear of the addiction, that he be given the will to follow through with the desire to reclaim his life. We separated. I left him there in the church alone with his own thoughts and woundedness. I will always remember his kneeling figure silhouetted against the altar. He was on his way back.

The other day Larry walked into the OMB office. He was clean from heroin, the result of detox and six months in a rehab center. He was a handsome man, and his face was full of hope and peace. He wanted to express his gratitude for what I had done, for my being with him in his time of crisis. I accepted the gift of gratitude even though I was aware that the praise belonged in another place, for surely he had been brought to me. I was only an instrument in a divine reality much bigger than the two of us.

■ ■ ■

I received word today from the grieving, long-suffering mother of Tanya that her daughter died last night, having never come out of her heroin-induced coma. Tanya was an old thirty-three. She had lived ten lives, if one wants to call what she was living "life": anger, depression, drugs, nutty liaisons, sugar daddies, sex, violence, misery, jail. I had seen her so whacked out that all she could do was stare and stumble. Many years ago, in a Tacoma drop-in center, she cut me up with a broken bottle. Paradoxically, that incident left us closer to each other.

Several months ago I visited Tanya in jail. She had been busted for prostitution, though I didn't think they would keep her for very long. At the time, it was undoubtedly the best place for her. She was not using dope and was receiving the proper medication for her bipolar condition, the latter having played hell with her for so long, constantly fueled by her drugging lifestyle. Gasoline and fire.

She was a handsome woman, possessing a tender heart, and was flat-out smart, with a mind that leaped like a leopard. But street drugs, in place of her medication, made her crazy, nasty, and mean. I know—I have a scar to prove it. She supported her habit most of the time by prostitution, specializing in poor and lonely elderly men who wanted to get laid and were willing to pay. By the time she had concluded the sexual end of business and had buttoned the last button, she usually had ripped off any valuable objects in the small apartment where the old fella lived. And sometimes, if the absentminded senior was intoxicated, she cleaned out his wallet. He wouldn't remember much about the encounter and would be too embarrassed to ask her about it. Tanya knew the ropes.

Frequently, the addict in withdrawal, especially one who sells sex, feels pervasive guilt in the absence of the drug. Off in the corner of one of the jail modules, Tanya talked to me, sometimes sobbing, trying to reconcile her longing for wholeness and the compulsions of destructive behavior. The guilt was thick and paralyzing, like a river of mud. It was disheartening, because there didn't seem to be a way out, short of a long-term regimen of treatment and counseling. I had seen her leave jails before and immediately plunge back into the river of ripping and running. Her judgment was impaired. She reminded me of a car in a demolition derby that repeatedly crashes into other cars. Finally, its engine and frame cracked and crushed, the car stops being a car and becomes a pile of scrap metal.

I loved Tanya very much. I understand why she died, but I do not understand the destructive forces that killed her. How often I wanted to sustain the little embraces we would give to each other, letting my tenderness seep into her body and soul and create a moment of trust. I wanted her to experience that peace where she could sink into herself and find that inner place that is God's peace, where there would be no strings attached, no deals, no propositions. Many nights, gathering up in my heart the people of the day, I asked God to work the miracle of good people in Tanya's life, to provide the rich self-understanding that would lead to a decent and happy life. It was not possible.

As I write this, I commend her and her momma to you, O God.

■ ■ ■

Funny, one of the most vivid memories I have of that day's chaos is of me sitting in my car in front of Mike's apartment, thinking how wacky the rest of the day might turn out to be. I was right. Mike had called the day before, told me that he was drinking again, and asked if I could come up to his place in southern Washington to talk. I had known him for several years from the streets and jails of Tacoma and Portland. After finishing his last jail sentence and staying free from alcohol, he resumed his education, and at the point of his call to me, he was within striking distance of an Associate in arts. He was smart and quick, which had enabled him to operate successfully in the seedy world of drug dealing and, in the case of school, had fueled his early conquests in the academic world. He earned a 4.0 in his first three semesters. He was even hatching a plan to enter a four-year school.

As I went into Mike's studio apartment that day, I entered the world of a human being's meltdown. After I knocked and he summoned me inside, I had to force the door open, since there was a turned-over table in front of it. The room smelled of sorrow and disappointment. I was looking at chaos: strewn furniture, beer cans, empty fifths of bourbon, full ashtrays, dirty dishes, broken lamps with their entrails hanging out, a broken bed. In short, it had suffered a direct hit that left rubble everywhere. There was a revolver in the kitchen sink. As my eyes focused in the darkened room, I saw Mike. He was a mess: flopped across the couch, one eye swollen shut, blood caked on his forehead and in his hair, his arm in a sling, and his face ravaged by sleeplessness and a tortured heart.

He had been in a fight the night before and had, as I subsequently found out, torn muscles in his right shoulder and a seriously injured eye. The long talk began, but as the day progressed, I realized the truth of "talking" to alcoholics: they will bob and weave through just about everything before they will confront their behavior. He rambled. He lied about so many things that I could not get a fix on the events that led to the relapse. Pressures of studies? A love affair that blew up? Depression? He had only vague memories of the altercation the night before in which he got his butt whipped so badly. And then there were the deeper issues connected with his history and early life, his drug using and dealing, and criminals from the past who had apparently resurfaced.

He had fallen in love. It had not only opened him up to some good and exciting growth and brought him happiness, but also, paradoxically, had unleashed some old demons. Can love do that? It was as if two movements were competing within him: loving being loved and believing he was unlovable. He kept using the word *monster* to describe himself, but did he call himself that because of some specific acts or because of delusions that were rooted in his self-loathing? Therein entered doubt, and confusion and fear bled into a relationship of potential goodness. Faced with it all, Mike broke off all contact with the woman, began to drink himself silly, and turned into, well, a monster. I thought to myself: *Are drugs far behind?*

The talk and the morning flew by, and I convinced him that we should go to the emergency room. That became my focus, getting him some medical assistance. I could have talked more in that trashed apartment, and subsequently in the emergency room, or at a restaurant, in the car—in short, I could have talked until I couldn't talk anymore, but all that talking would have been futile, because he was not listening. My sense was that all he really wanted was another drink, and I was a safe person to have around while he meandered through his thoughts. He actually sneaked a couple shots of whiskey while I was making some phone calls during a restaurant stop on our return from the hospital.

After driving back from the hospital, I told Mike that I was not going to be drawn into his mess any further. If he wanted to get sober, then he knew what he had to do, or I would be glad to give him references. But that was it. I would not be used.

Driving back to Portland, I could only pray that Mike would learn to see himself as God sees him, that he would realize how helpless he was, how liquor was again cutting a destructive swath across his life, and that the only answer was recognizing this and entrusting himself to the higher power. I prayed for myself, too, that I would have the capacity to be ruthlessly honest with him.

He called a year later. He said that he had waited out a year of sobriety before he called me. It touched me. I told him I was glad that he was OK and suggested that sometime we get together if he ever came to Portland. My last words to him were that I loved him and believed in him.

I didn't hear from him again until another year had passed. I received in the mail a copy of his diploma from a four-year school in Washington. Not only was he alive, but he had also finished school with a GPA of 3.87. He had been sober since that awful day. What a welcome stunner. Dead and now alive. He sent a note of thanks with his diploma, said he was grateful that God had believed in him through me. I do believe in him, even as I know that the alcoholic is only a drink away from destruction.

Thank you, O God, for your "power, working in us, [which] can do infinitely more than we can ask or imagine" (Ephesians 3:20).

chapter six

TO LOVE AND BE LOVED:

RELATIONSHIPS IN THE STREETS

I have seen love flourish among the people I serve,
where the happiness of the beloved was all that
mattered. Such love is not easy, but it exists and
reminds me constantly of that divine spark in all
of us that invites us to love and be loved.

This afternoon I stopped off to
see Johnny at his hotel. Also present were Marilyn and Clarice.
Everyone was a little plastered. All in their fifties, going on ninety.
Here was the shock of the day: Johnny and Marilyn have a thing
going. It was strange to see their little acts of affection, like the flir-
tations of two love-struck teenagers.

What is love on the streets and in the SROs? I always have to
look twice when I see it, as though I've come across some species of
animal that I never dreamed could exist in this country. And yet
there it is. The disbelief is not that love is there but that it could

find a toehold in the inhospitable atmosphere of the SRO, saturated as it is with loneliness and human impoverishment, heartache and alienation. But there it is, in all its giddiness and freshness, with accompanying overtures of constant love and protestations of loyalty. Of course, in the case of Johnny and Marilyn, it is fragile, because of that quicksand of relationships, alcoholism. That is very unsettling for me because I care for the two of them.

Like the flowers that grow in the sidewalk cracks in Old Town, some extraordinary loves have come into being and have thrived in the world of the streets and the SROs. If it is the real deal, then it has moved past environment and backgrounds and age and has arrived at selflessness. Like the torrid romances of celebrities, which often burn out like meteors, the love affairs down here often fizzle, because the lovers have self-centered agendas. But I have seen love flourish among the people I serve, where the happiness of the beloved was all that mattered. Such love is not easy, but it exists and reminds me constantly of that divine spark in all of us that invites us to love and be loved.

■ ■ ■

John and Judy, both in their forties, had been together for more than ten years when I met them. Those ten-plus years were drenched in the vicissitudes of the streets, which would destroy most relationships. John was tall, with a big shock of well-kept hair, graying prematurely; intense eyes; and a smile that appeared rarely but, when it did, transformed his face like Christmas lights transform a tree. He held down jobs off and on as a musician and a clerk. He was an alcoholic who would go on colossal benders. When he did, he and Judy would split up, and he would wind up in detox for yet another try at sobriety.

Judy was small, almost frail, with a shy demeanor and a good and loving heart. She had a disability and therefore received a sustenance check each month. She was also helped out by her aging parents, who had money. She had a history of drug abuse. Both partners possessed insecurities that I always thought would erode, if not destroy, their relationship. There were lots of split-ups. He was bossy and demanding. They were codependent and yet were not. Neither one of them was a saint. It seemed that if their insecurity didn't guarantee a dead end in the world of love, then the drugs and liquor would.

One afternoon John informed me that Judy had been diagnosed with a virulent form of bone cancer, and it appeared to be metastasizing quickly. Chemo and radiation had commenced, but the prognosis was not good. Eventually, the doctors told her that she had only a few months to live. Because she was deteriorating so rapidly and because she needed constant care, she was moved to a hospice foster home. It was a long haul for John, those months. And a longer one for Judy.

Each day, John would hop on a city bus and make the hour trip out to see her. I began to get a sense of the depth of his devotion: he was focused, aware, his entire self directed toward the woman he loved, who was dying on the other side of town. In the crisis that lasted several months, he never drank a drop.

He asked me one morning if I could come out and pray with them and anoint her with oil, the sacrament of the sick. With a hitch in his voice, his gaunt face looking directly at me, he told me that he thought the end was near.

We entered the hospice, a foster home that contained four extra rooms for the sick. As we stepped into her room, I thought we had taken a wrong turn, because we were clearly in the room of a withering-away senior who looked to be a hundred. It was Judy.

Her eyes and her weak voice greeted me. Her frail body was barely detectable beneath the covers. She was bald, toothless, thin, withered. I couldn't take my eyes off her translucent eyes. There was no hesitation, no guile, nothing but appreciative and attentive awareness of our presence.

John went to her, leaned over her, and kissed her and stroked her forehead. As he held her hands, I offered a prayer and then anointed her forehead, neck, and hands. I read the Twenty-third Psalm.

John never took his eyes off her, his face simultaneously reflecting a look of unspeakable love and the weariness of a long and exhausting journey. Judy was very ill, so I did not linger long. Before I left, I prayed once again and then kissed her on her chilled forehead. I felt she would die that night. As John was preparing to walk me to the door, he bent over and took her into his arms, as she did him, reaching her emaciated arms up and around this man with whom she had spent so much of her life and who was walking with her, being with her, supporting her, relentlessly loving her to the very end. It was an embrace as tender and gentle as I have ever seen.

Judy died the next morning, in the arms of her beloved.

∎ ∎ ∎

As I rode back on the bus after my last visit with Judy, I remembered a poor elderly couple I visited in San Diego, Cora and Wiley. It was the summer after I was ordained a Jesuit priest, and I was working in a parish.

Wiley was in bad shape: blind, immobile, sick with diabetes, his legs amputated. As I was concluding my visit, I looked at him and thought, *What a mess this guy is.* At that very moment, Cora folded her arms, gazed at him, then at me, then back at him, saying, "God, I love that man."

I think it was my first real lesson in what beauty consists of.

The reasons we love, really love, a person have nothing to do with appearance. They have everything to do with our heart and the heart of the beloved. Nurses know this, as do mothers and fathers and spouses who are in it for the long haul. God sends people like Cora and Wiley into my life to remind me of this, allows me to witness John and Judy's version of the same truth. As the Little Prince said, "What is essential is invisible to the eye." The heart of God sees what is essential.

I have seen my share of love affairs on the streets. Some have come and gone peacefully, like a morning rainfall; some have wound up on the junk pile of unfaithfulness; some devolved into anger and shouting matches; some were abandoned in the name of that more possessive lover, drugs; some ended with one lover killing the other; some were cut down in the initial flush because one of the two died. And some flourished, the lovers having embraced the qualities of selflessness and compassion that come out of hard-won love. As an outside observer, I admire and cherish these examples of enduring love.

■ ■ ■

I had done the intake on James when he came to Outreach Ministry. He was in his early sixties at the time and had hit the wall after a lifetime of alcohol and drug abuse. He had cleaned up only to find out that he had cancer. He was a man of great personal pride, always neat and orderly in appearance. He had burned most of the bridges in his life, including those with a former wife and their daughter. As methodical as he was in telling me his story, I could see that he bore a lot of pain over lost love and huge doses of guilt over his neglect of those he loved, both when he was using drugs and afterward.

I went to visit him once when he was in the hospital, early in our relationship, and he told me that he would like to see his daughter. Could I help him out? At the time, he was in the psych ward, struggling with the wrong combination of chemotherapy and medication and having a fleeting but frightening psychotic episode. He sat there with tears in his eyes, talking about his daughter, fidgeting in his hospital gown, wearing a San Francisco 49ers baseball cap.

Eventually I was able to arrange a conference with James, his daughter, and his former wife. His ex had insisted that I be there. The reunion occurred in a small deli over turkey sandwiches and Sprites. James's teenage daughter was a lovely person, very intelligent like her parents and shy, as was to be expected under the circumstances. She wanted to meet and get to know her dad.

At the outset the conversation was disquieting because James was rambling nervously, whining about how one couldn't smoke "in this damn place." I wanted to clobber him. When he had to use the restroom, I followed him.

Once I got him alone, I let him have it: "My God, James, this is your daughter, and she is here to see *you*. Stop blabbing so much and listen to her and find out something of her heart. It's painful and intimidating enough to know that your dad is a junkie and an alcoholic and is dying of cancer. So get with it, man."

The truth of what I said was so obvious that he could only shake his head and say, "You're so goddamn right, Father."

The rest of the visit went well, and Susan, James's daughter, revealed herself to be a timid but engaging person.

There were more deli visits, and eventually we switched to meeting at his subsidized apartment. In most cases, everyone felt better if I was there. At one point, after James announced that he had purchased the complete works of James Joyce, his daughter asked James to talk about Joyce. The son of a gun launched into a tour-de-force analysis of Joyce, his history and his writings. It was astonishing—like discovering a beautiful and enchanting subterranean lake. He may have been dying of cancer, but intellectually he had not lost his touch.

Near the end of his life, James would come into the office in the morning. We would chat, and he would ask to be anointed. One day he came by to announce to me that his younger sister had died suddenly in northern California. He was wounded, and he wept intensely. "I just didn't expect it, I just didn't expect it," he sobbed, as one who had suffered a loss beyond anything a bystander could grasp. He had maintained such composure during all the chemo and blood transfusions and medications, but this news unraveled him. He had never reconciled with his sister, and now it was too late—at least in this life.

When the cancer precipitated a form of dementia that left him very forgetful, his social worker decided to move him to a locked-down care facility. Such a move was impossible for the independent part of him to grasp. He was furious and "pissed off" about the facility. Hated it. Whenever I visited him he would make disparaging comments about the staff. Yet he was very disoriented; it was the only safe place where he could receive the care he needed.

The night before he died, Laurie and I went over to see him, and I anointed him. His ex-wife and daughter were present and would be there until the end. The last thing he said to me was "Oh, Father," which I took to be both an utterance of frustration and an expression of gratitude for our presence. He died that night with his family at his bedside.

I woke up at four o'clock the next morning. James was on my mind, and my sense was that he was probably gone. Lots of memories emerged: the long talks, his concern for me when I went to El Salvador and his fear of "those goddamn armies killing Jesuits," and his pride when he told me that he had willed all of his books to his daughter, including his beloved James Joyce collection. I prayed for him as I lay there in bed.

My God, into your hands I commend his spirit. Forgive him his failures; embrace him for all that was good in him. Remember what his wife said: "He was a force in our lives." What a remarkable thing to say. Bless her. Bless their daughter.

■ ■ ■

There are two faces of grief worn by the partners of those who die: one is the face of emptiness that comes with the loss of the beloved, and the other is the face of fear precipitated by the reality of going it alone. I saw both looks today at the memorial service for Carlene, who had gotten clean at last from drugs but then died suddenly. Heart attack.

She was fifty. The grief of her man, James, showed how absolutely nuts he was about her. She died in his arms. *In his arms.* What would it be like to lose your beloved so suddenly? And what if it was someone to whom you had committed yourself, who had shared what is best and most human about you?

The memorial service went well, held together by the love of the families and friends of Carlene and James.

I officiated at another memorial service today for thirty-six-year-old George, dead of a heroin overdose. The people in attendance included his girlfriend, Kathy; two of his former wives and three of his four children; and assorted friends, most of them ex-users, several in treatment. It was, as these events always are, a time full of sadness and pathos for the people who live in the world of drugs.

The most pathetic part of it all was the sense of loss and waste. Here was a guy who apparently had won the love of so many people, who had begun to connect with his kids. And yet in one brain-hijacked moment, he blew it all with a slam of dope into his arm in an obscure back street phone booth. And the children: how will they ever get over it? Even if they do, they will live a life deprived of a father.

There were lots of tears. I was struck by the power of the love and attention that friends bring to these occasions. I tried, as I always do when I know absolutely no one at the service, to simply be the bridge over troubled waters, letting people talk about their experience of the deceased. May he rest in peace.

■ ■ ■

I was at the Nestucca Sanctuary retreat house on the coast, sorting my heart out. The night before I left town, I had a long talk with a fellow whose girlfriend had died suddenly. They lived together in an SRO. Theirs was a simple and honest love—a love, I think, that was born of the suffering in their respective lives, which enabled them to appreciate the honest love of another as a precious gift. This gift surpassed everything else, bad or good, in their lives. Their greatest desire was to love each other.

Desire. Isn't that all that really matters? The desire to love and be loved and the desire to know and love God, who is the author of such all-encompassing desire. And emerging from this truth are all these other desires that drive my life: the desire to understand life, the desire to be faithful to the love I have for those I most cherish, the desire to be a Jesuit who has interior knowledge of his vocation, the desire to find my life with the poor, and the desire to passionately live and preach the gospel.

I thank the One who fills me with desire . . . and who desires me.

chapter seven

STREET SCENES:

GLIMPSES OF OLD TOWN

> The poor teach me that serving them is not just
> some sort of Christian imperative. Rather,
> it is in serving them that I can discover,
> like the church, what is best in my own heart.

Part of my wholeness and sanity comes from maintaining a healthy exercise regimen, which for the most part involves early morning runs along the Willamette River, about half a mile from my residence. I ran very early today, wanting to beat the holiday crowd at Riverfront Park. About halfway through my run, at one of the more scenic sections overlooking the river, I came upon several police cars, an emergency service car, an ambulance—and a crowd. At first I thought it was an early security setup for the anticipated holiday throngs, but as I neared the scene, I realized that there were no park personnel around.

The cops were fishing a body out of the river.

I stopped and stared with the rest of the hushed bystanders. On the dock, in an unzipped body bag on a police stretcher, they placed a blanched and bloated male body. I heard a policeman say that the victim had been shot.

Seeing dead bodies is not a new thing for me; what struck me was the casual and frivolous attitude of the police around the unknown corpse. It baffled me. Then I corrected myself: *Loosen up, Gary. Better for them to chuckle a little during such a thankless job than to throw up on the sidewalk.*

These men and women see a lot more death than I do in the course of their work. As I continued to run, I whispered prayers for this brother. Shot to death. Dumped in the Willamette.

■ ■ ■

These were some of the things I saw as I was running through the predawn streets this morning, in weather that was one degree below freezing: a woman sleeping on a bench in front of a bank, her grocery cart stuffed so high that it created a wall between the bench and the rest of the sidewalk; nearing the waterfront, an army of rats—somehow "pack" does not say it—pouring out of a vacant building toward a pile of bread crumbs left by a pigeon lover; four people, sleeping body to body, under the Morrison Street Bridge; Dave, a street friend, waving silently to me down on the riverfront as he checked for redeemable cans in the trash containers, like a raccoon hunting for food; a lightly dressed woman foraging for cigarette butts in an ashtray by Starbucks; two intoxicated men with blankets pulled around their shoulders arguing over a bottle of booze, one with a urine stain on his pants; a solitary person lying on the heating grate on the sidewalk in front of the "Telephone Building"; a small group of young men, drug dealers, waiting on the corner across from where I live. It was about time for the early morning crack and marijuana hunters to make their furtive appearance. One of the dealers greeted me as I zoomed by: "Morning, Pastor."

■ ■ ■

Phil boarded the number nine bus with me, drinking some concoction of wine and coke. He is an old street friend whom I first met years ago at the jail and who moves from one hotel to the next. He has an extraordinarily friendly and open demeanor, and he clearly likes me because of the jail connection and because I always talk with him when we encounter each other on the street. We sat next to each other on the bus, and he regaled me with stories of the things going on in his life. We roamed through topics: his past ("I was dumped by my mom and raised by the state of California"), his addiction ("I have dealers who will loan me a lot, and I have fought and shot some that have screwed me"), his desire to write ("Got four pregnant files of notes about my life"), his girlfriends ("I love heavy women"), and his faith ("I am lucky to be alive; I have been cut and shot and beaten and overdosed. Maybe God keeps me alive to be an example to the rest of these assholes").

The bus was beginning to fill up, and at one point Phil, not missing a beat in his conversation, got up and directed an elderly woman to take his place. She did, trying not to listen to our conversation. But this was no easy job, since Phil, his long, lean body hanging over her and the tattoo on his biceps wriggling in her face, was fearlessly peppering the conversation with references to his love life, his criminal record, his curiosity about me, and information on the latest preacher he had heard and wanted me to meet.

I tried to imagine her later, possibly over coffee with a friend, trying to describe that conversation and its strange participants.

The bus became so packed that Phil, still standing, was pushed back a few seats. In the semisilence of a bus full of tired workers heading home, he asked loud and strong, "How long you been a priest, Gary?"

The heads turned to look at the phenomenon of a real live priest, as if there were a giraffe on board.

"Since 1971," I responded.

Phil: "I am going to say this before God and you and the whole bus: You are one bad dude."

The people on the bus applauded. What a show: God as a witness, a giraffe-like priest, and an outrageous extrovert from the streets. Not your everyday cast of characters on the late-afternoon and dreary number nine.

We got off together and gabbed a bit about another great minister he had heard recently. "Now this guy preaches the word. You'd like him." He embraced me with his big, gangly body and was off down the street.

Yep, that's me: one bad dude.

■ ■ ■

How strange to look out my window last night at nine o'clock and see swarms of men clad in black FBI jackets closing off the streets. It was a drug sweep, and the FBI agents were accompanied by local law enforcement people, who also had their identity plastered on their backs. Street people were being stopped and many were being arrested without too much discussion. The sweepers had reams of photographs and clearly knew who they were looking for. It was like an invasion of aliens who knew the turf and possessed absolute control. Isn't it strange: people who have never lived here coming among us with such power?

Most of those arrested were Hispanics. The majority of heroin dealers here are Mexican and Central American youth, far from home, living by their wits on the street and surviving by selling dope.

"What will this child become?" asked Elizabeth's neighbors about the child who would become John the Baptist. Did a Mexican momma and daddy and all their neighbors once—in hope—ask this same question when a babe was born in some obscure village, the same child now on the streets of Portland, tracked down and arrested by the police? A babe then, now caught up in the tentacles of drugs and the relentless power of drug enforcement.

■ ■ ■

Cal hailed me last night as I was walking past the bank. His face was battered, the result of being jumped by thugs. His nose was broken and his mouth was pretty badly cut up. He will have a couple of bad-looking shiners. He was robbed of three hundred dollars, essentially his rent money for next month, so he is on the streets again. The poor guy is lost when it comes to the practicalities of life. He has limited intelligence, and on top of that, he suffers from a learning disability that was not diagnosed until late in his childhood. I have known him for years, have seen him do his time in jail and kick drugs (I think he has been clean for two years now), and have been a beneficiary of his loyalty, his childlike goodness, and his friendship.

He once said to me, "You are the only father I have ever had." He never knew his real father—the only father figures he had were his mother's lovers, who had emotionally tossed him to the wind like a cigarette butt out the car window. I do care for him, and I understand the gaps in his life thanks to my own experience of growing up with a severe and demanding stepfather. Cal has had to overcome many obstacles. In these moments with him, when evil men have taken advantage of him, I think of those lines from Isaiah, which are applicable to many of the individuals of the streets who must grow up and try to make it in a country of instability:

> *Flying backward and forward*
> *like bewildered nestlings.*
>
> ISAIAH 16:2

■ ■ ■

Among the poor, the church learns to be indignant at the sight of discarded human beings, and it is taught to passionately challenge systems and structures that produce such human beings. It is one thing to practice charity, to give a poor person some bread or to treat the same person with respect. It is quite another thing to challenge a system in which people are hungry, in which some can be so rich and many are poor. As Cardinal Sin of the Philippines once said: "Love without justice is baloney."

It is true that the church must be in many places and with many people, but it is the poor who will reveal to the church—dramatically and poignantly—the nature of its heart and mission.

The Gospels and the documents of the church speak directly to the notion of solidarity with the poor. Books have been written on it. Sermons have been preached on it. But the poor themselves instruct me in the practical realities of this notion. I find out about them by entering their world. Solidarity with them means knowing them, their sights and smells and sounds, their hopes and deprivations.

The poor teach me that serving them is not just some sort of Christian imperative. Rather, it is in serving them that I can discover, like the church, what is best in my own heart.

■ ■ ■

A few days ago, as I was getting into my car, a hooker approached me. She was young and a bit nervous as she asked me if I "wanted a date." I looked into her face, which had a sad, pleading quality about it. Another name: despair.

"What's your price?"

"Depends on what you want."

"I'll give you twenty bucks to just sit in the car and talk with me."

A trick who wanted only to talk: a creature from another planet. She smiled, a sort of what's-the-scam-here look on her face. She got in. I gave her the twenty and told her who I was.

"Can I ask you something?" I asked.

"Depends, but it's your money. What do you want to know? You sure you're a priest?"

"How come you are so unhappy?"

She looked at me, her eyes filled with tears, and then she looked down at her hands, which were nervously folding and unfolding the twenty. Out of the corner of my eye I could see her pimp watching from an adjacent park, trying to figure out what the hell was going on. "It's a long story. Can we talk again at some other time?"

We made arrangements to meet at a local coffee joint the next day. She got out of the car, reached back through the window, handed me the twenty, and walked into the park.

■ ■ ■

Street women involved in prostitution. It is a heavy thought. As a man, I am ashamed. These women are the playgrounds and dumps of sexual aberrations and the victims of our culture's obsession with indifferent, anonymous sex and male power. It is important for the church to be there with these sisters and offer them a concrete opportunity to see who they really are: not chunks of meat, but images of the heart of God. We have to offer them, gently, the freedom they all deserve, through safe options and opportunities.

I take it all personally. If a woman or a man is abused, then I am abused, and if I don't feel that way, then I want to feel that way. If your flesh is lacerated, so is mine.

> *God has arranged the body so that more dignity is*
> *given to the parts which are without it, and so that*
> *there may not be disagreements inside the body, but*
> *that each part may be equally concerned for all the*
> *others. If one part is hurt, all parts are hurt with it.*
> 1 CORINTHIANS 12:24–26

■ ■ ■

I did a stupid thing the other night. I decided to take a shortcut back to the chapel at about eleven o'clock at night in an effort to get home a little earlier. I rounded the corner in a poorly lit area, and there, hanging out, were two guys. Instinctively I knew I was in trouble. As I walked briskly past them, one of them asked if I had any marijuana. (Right. Like I look like a dealer.) I threw "nope" over my shoulder and kept on moving.

He then ordered me to stop and said threateningly, "Come here, man."

I picked up my pace as he started yelling at me. The voice got closer, and I turned to see the two of them coming after me, one carrying a tire iron and saying, "I'm going to fuck you up." I took off running, knowing that I was about half a block from a main street, lots of traffic, and plenty of ever-lovin' light.

They pulled up as I made it safely to my goal, breathing hard, my heart pounding. I was scared. And pissed off. I was hit by the sickness of it all, of their total indifference to our shared humanity. They would have hit me and robbed me as the blood pumped through their veins and dropped from their lips. Like squashing a bug. In such moments, I am looking at cold-blooded evil.

■ ■ ■

One Saturday night, two men started a shoving match below my third-floor window. It was just one of a million in-your-face confrontations that occur in the throes of the street. Like usual, it was all machismo and shouting. Suddenly one man pulled a knife, and I was looking down at a new and perilous situation. The potential victim then shouted at the knife wielder, in a voice that echoed off the tall buildings and over the 2 A.M. traffic noises, "You can't kill me, motherfucker. I'm already dead." The "dead" man, whom I see periodically as he moves among the dope dealers, turned his back on the knife wielder and walked away into the night.

There are lots of self-perceived dead people walking around on the streets. Society has names for all the nameless brothers and sisters of the night: addicts, bums, panhandlers, crackheads, hookers, wackos. Many consider themselves dead because no one ever told them about the beauty of their lives.

As I tried to sleep that night, I thought of the small replica I have of Rembrandt's *Prodigal Son,* the kneeling returned son weeping in the arms of his father. And later, the same father said to his other son, "Your brother here was dead and has come to life; he was lost and is found" (Luke 15:32).

I determined to snag the dead man if I saw him again and take a shot at exploring life with him. How could I not try?

■ ■ ■

One evening I was waiting on the corner of Broadway and Burnside, looking, I suppose, a bit disconcerted and needy. I was going to a very heavy meeting where there would be lots of conflict. As I waited for my ride, two Bible-packing, perpetually smiling, glazed-eyed gentlemen approached me. They hit on me, so to speak.

One of them asked me, "Do you like Mexican food, brother?"

"Sure," I responded. "You looking for a restaurant?"

"Oh, gosh, no," he said. They both guffawed.

Turns out that they were in the hunt for people they could take in their van to their church for a meal of burritos, tamales, and tacos. With, I presume, evangelization for dessert.

I turned them down, looking nervously for my ride.

At that point I was given the consolation prize: one of them put his hand on my shoulder and said, with the smarmy assurance that only "The Saved" seem to have down cold, "It's okay, brother, Jesus still loves you."

Yeah, you are right, my friend, Jesus does love me, but the means and story of that love are so different from anything you can imagine.

I guess I will never trust these guys because they are here today and gone tomorrow, and the poor need consistency of commitment. I don't doubt their sincerity of intention. But there is a tendency among some religious groups to analyze life on the streets—and the response to that life—in simplistic terms. This is not a quick-fix world, despite God's power. And when the poor don't get it right away—that is, that sweet Jesus loves them—the born-againers leave the scene, shaking the dust from their feet. Rather than listening to the Spirit in the poor, these proselytizers listen to their own safe, untested selves and to their own self-congratulatory gospel of salvation. In doing so they miss the bruised hearts of others. They miss, I think, the heart of Jesus, so complex, open, and long-suffering.

■ ■ ■

I was awakened at 5 A.M. by the not unusual sound of screaming police sirens. Normally they race past our chapel residence, but this time they stopped. I went to the window and looked out onto the street, where I could see several police officers, now out of their squad cars, surrounding a knife-wielding man in front of a local mom-and-pop store. He was naked.

At one point the police started shooting rubber bullets at him: one, two, three, four, five shots. The man began to howl in pain and fell to the sidewalk, where he was subdued by the officers.

Apparently this naked man was attempting to break into the store and had set off a silent alarm. As the police officers were placing him into one of the cars, I was weighed down by the sadness of it all: a mentally deranged human being, lost, whose life at that point had been reduced to hunger, nakedness, and the pain of police bullets. He was like a wounded animal, seeking refuge but not having a clue of where to find it.

■ ■ ■

This morning, as I was making a newspaper run down Broadway Avenue, I ran into Red, a tall, amiable guy who lives here and there and has a history of drug abuse. We chatted briefly, and he told me that he was trying to launch a music career. He said he did great imitations of singers. Would I like to hear some?

Sure, Red, it's a little weird auditioning you here on Burnside and Sixth at 7:30 in the morning, but what the hell. It certainly was no problem for him; the place and the audience did not make much difference. What counted was the opportunity to show what he had. Red gave me a great little concert, imitating the melodious tones of Johnny Mathis, Nat King Cole, and Engelbert Humperdinck. He was pretty good—more for style than imitation—and his smile got bigger as he knocked down each singer. It was a remarkable private concert, Red belting out the songs and waving at any honking cars.

■ ■ ■

Today was a blitz day.

I came to the Outreach Ministry office and had to argue a couple off the front steps, where they had slept on a cardboard mattress the night before.

Then I took an earful of abuse from Andy, who walked in behind my back, very drunk and red faced with fury, and chewed me out over all the money I had stolen from him. (Where does all that fury come from, I wonder, and will he one day be unable to express it with words and simply strangle me?)

Laurie, an OMB staffer, and I talked over our game plan for the day, since we were missing a staff person; while we were talking, there was a car accident on the corner in front of the office. We offered our phone to one of the weeping drivers, who held a young child in each arm.

Later on, as I was heading over to Sisters of the Road Café, a nonprofit restaurant for the poor in Old Town, several people tried to sell me drugs (I've got that look of a voracious addict). I bumped into Too Fat Bruce (his appellation for himself), and he informed me that he was returning to school for a master's in social work, a reformed druggie in spades.

While the droning bump-and-grind music from a twenty-four-hour strip joint on the bottom floor of an SRO was rising through the building, I spoke with a hotel manager about a woman who had disappeared. I stopped off to see Arnie, but he was too drunk and miserable to talk. Then I stood in the hallway of the third floor of the same hotel, talking with Nancy, aware that I was drowning in the sounds of TVs and radios and people yelling plus the smell of urine and feces and vomit and billions of cigarettes and new paint over old walls.

I broke up a potential fight in the lobby of the chapel between two women (they wanted to punch me out after it was all over); traveled with Mara to visit Cliff at the Hatfield, where he broke down and cried over his happiness at having someone visit him ("You are angels," he exclaimed to us); and officiated at a memorial service for a woman who had overdosed.

At the end of the day, I asked the Holy Spirit to be with me and with all the people of the day, to comfort us with strength and love.

■ ■ ■

I spent one morning walking in the forest park that overlooks northwest Portland. I needed to breathe some different air.

Friends were on my mind. More than ever, I was feeling the absence of friends who lived far away and gratitude for friends who were part of my life here. They are at the heart of one of life's greatest mysteries.

There are moments when I think my powers are no longer adequate to handle my problems. When I ask God for help and comfort in these moments, it often comes in the shape of a person. This reminds me of one of my favorite lines from Scripture: "[God] comforted us, by the arrival of Titus" (2 Corinthians 7:6).

Those friends in my life whom I cherish and who cherish me are channels of God's love and power. When God has comforted me, it has occasionally been through an idea or a prayer, but it has more often been through the touch and care of a friend, as Titus gave to Paul.

Martin Buber says that we are created along with one another and directed to a life with one another and that by means of our brother and sister creatures we find our way to God. Man, is that ever true of me. My friends have been the ones who have pulled me through some absolutely awful moments, and they have been the people in whose presence I have found my most delirious moments of happiness.

Friends have nurtured me, cajoled me, wept over me, breathed on me when I thought I was dead; they walked with me in the early days of my studies and have walked with me in my ministry; they have been there to celebrate my victories and have held me in their arms when I was running on empty. In a word, my friends have loved me. One grows in the presence of love. Here is the mystery: God gets hold of things and people and uses them to bring me to life. Therein lies another mystery: I too am a channel of God's comfort for all whom God will bring into my life.

As I wandered the trails, a few favorite lines of my friend Lynn Martin's wonderful poem "Prayer" came to mind, in which she expresses her prayerful hopes for a friend:

I wanted your winters
in the future to be easy, with enough
coal for the fire. I want the world
to open up its shutters for you, to be
sky and rain and space, for the wind
to bring you birds, hundreds of birds.

■ ■ ■

I came around a corner one night long ago, and there was Shea, drunk as a skunk, on his knees, marooned on a corner, holding on to a lamppost. A mounted policeman was there, apparently waiting for the pickup van from the detox center. I stopped, identified myself to the officer, and tried to engage Shea in a conversation. But he was fascinated by the horse and announced that he would like to kiss her. I guess those big, fat horse lips were too irresistible. The horse stared back with a look of total boredom. She had seen his kind before.

Shea was a short, grizzly bearded man with twinkly blue eyes, pushing seventy. He had been in Old Town forever. He was born and raised in Illinois, one of several brothers and sisters. When he was growing up, he worked with his father as a stonemason, eventually leaving home to make it on his own. He spent time as a ranch hand in Colorado and Wyoming and as a member of the military during the Korean War. There were many years in Portland, where he did a variety of jobs until his age and disabilities prevented him from working (muggers had at one time broken his hips in a robbery attempt).

Shea was the gift giver. One way or another, Outreach Ministry and its staff were the beneficiaries of his unique talent for finding discarded things that his friends might be able to use. He collected his stash of things from the streets, from dumpsters, from parks, from the entire territory that constituted his wandering area. He usually earmarked a "find" for a specific staff person: a plastic garbage container for a car (for Dorothy); a little handheld plastic gadget used by baseball umpires to keep track of balls, strikes, and outs (for me); an army of figurines and knickknacks for Peg's cubby hole of an office; a *Cosmopolitan* magazine written in

Russian (for Laurie, who speaks no Russian); children's books (for Kathy's granddaughter). He used to bring in every free newspaper he could lay his hands on until we stopped him from doing so. During a period of time in which I was whining about our lousy vacuum cleaner, he walked in with a beat-up beauty he found in a dumpster. The bottom plate was gone, and the noise drove us all nuts ("Give it some oil," he commanded), but the darn thing worked. He was the human magnet; nothing escaped him.

Shea had suffered. He knew better than most about life's ups and downs, its misunderstandings and broken relationships. He had endured the disorder of internal battles and physical disabilities. He came through it all not as a bitter, cantankerous, and introverted old man but as a human being capable of a loving response to those he trusted. Of course, like all of us, he had his moments of grumpiness and orneriness, but they would dissolve quickly in the arms of a hugger. Tough looking on the outside, he was caramel on the inside, and this was no more evident than when he held a small child in his arms.

Never making a big deal about his actions, Shea captured what Outreach seeks to realize in itself, which *is* a big deal. As a ministry, we are more than money managers; he reminded us that we are a family—a family of friends—which most of our members never had. We understand that real care for the poor and the little people of the world means being in love for the long haul. Shea's longevity at OMB testified to that fact. We tried to walk with him: through the laughs, the pain and injuries, the gifts, the hugs, and the dizzying battles of old age. Right on to death. In turn, he walked with Outreach Ministry, teaching us and the people of Old Town about the possibilities of love and faithfulness.

chapter eight

GO IN PEACE:

CELEBRATING MASS IN OLD TOWN

> I realize that God brought me into this world,
> blessed with skills and talents. The only thing that
> makes sense to me is to use them in the service of
> the poor. It is at their feet that I find myself.

There is a Mass every evening at the Downtown Chapel, one that is attended, for the most part, by folks from the SROs, a few local businesspeople who have just gotten off work, and people who come from other parts of the city because they want to attend an evening Mass. Often street folks wander in to check things out.

You never know what is going to happen.

One evening Shane went off. Well, sort of. He is a young man who has been on the streets for as long as I can remember. He is about thirty, has schizophrenia, is achingly good-looking, moves furtively, and is loaded to the gills with anger. He is suspicious of everyone, and when he talks with me, it is usually a rambling, nonstop discourse on the abuses that have been heaped upon him by everyone, from society in general to the manager of the local rescue mission. He denies he has any mental illness and verbally attacks me when I move the conversation to the topic of getting him assistance. Periodically he will inform me that he no longer wants to talk to me and that I should not even acknowledge him on the streets. I have seen him scurrying down the street on cold and rainy days, all his belongings in a plastic garbage bag slung over his shoulder, like a river rat popping up from the depths. It breaks my heart.

This particular night, before Mass, he and another street person, Jeff, had a minor altercation in the second-floor bathroom of the church. It was primarily a verbal exchange with a couple of shoves thrown in. Jeff is a nervous Nellie who also suffers from mental illness and, like Shane, survives. He eventually came to Mass, while Shane, furious, sulking and steaming, remained in the lobby of the church. Until the first reading of Scripture. At that point, he entered the church and walked along the side wall, clearly headed in my direction. I was seated, piously listening to the first Scripture reading, but I spotted him out of the corner of my eye. I knew that when he was in a paranoid state, he could be prone to the occasional punch.

He stopped at the front of the church, but off to the side of the sanctuary, and said to me—while the lector was reading—that he had to see me outside in the lobby. Weighing the odds that I might be able to cool him down out there and prevent one of his rambling discourses in the church, I decided to move to the lobby with him. I thought that I could quickly convince him to hold it for a while until I had time to talk. When we reached the lobby, Shane turned to me and began to call Jeff every version of "motherfucker" I had ever heard, with a few juicy modifiers thrown in for emphasis.

I gauged my time and told him that I would see him after Mass; could he wait? Yes, you're damn right he could.

Unfortunately for the assembled parishioners, I had forgotten to turn off my body microphone. During the first reading, they were simultaneously blessed by the holy word of God and blasted by the salty word of Shane.

It wasn't over. I read the Gospel, felt the oratorical wheels come off my distracted homily, and finished just as Shane decided to come in. He marched up before the bewildered congregation and the bewildered celebrant and began to show everyone his track-free arms, especially Jeff, who had apparently accused Shane of being a drug addict during the infamous bathroom altercation. Jeff, of course, became upset with me, because I had allowed Shane to interrupt Mass. His point made, Shane stomped out. I was pretty jittery during the rest of the Mass, waiting for a sniper attack.

The next day Jeff approached me as I was moving through the lobby of the chapel and heading outside. *Could we talk, Father?* He wanted to make a confession. I said okay, but my gut was telling me to be careful. I took him into the poorly lit chapel, thinking it would be a quiet place yet visible through glass doors to the outside lobby. We sat in one of the pews near the door. He was agitated, sweat beading on his upper lip. Then he broke into a paranoid story of people from New Zealand invading our country and driving everyone south, all the time assuring me that he was not mentally ill, as "you, Father Gary, had allowed Shane to insinuate yesterday." I became nervous when he said that he had something to give me, a gift for a person he admired and loved. I was on high alert. As he reached into a small brown paper bag he had brought with him and had left sitting ominously next to him, I was expecting him to pull out a weapon. It was too late to make a run for it; I'd have been plugged in the back. I steeled myself, my right arm resting behind him on the back of the pew. I figured at that point that, should he pull out a weapon, I could either grab his arm or land one good punch. Slowly his hand came out of the bag.

And he pulled out a bouquet of pansies.

"For you, Father, for being so patient with Shane and me yesterday."

Two men, two human beings, both very sick. It always brings me to my knees. I thought of the words of Abraham Heschel: "When I see a man . . . I see the only entity in nature with which sanctity is associated. The particular individual may not be dear to me—in fact, I may even dislike him. But he is dear to someone else, to his mother, for example, although that, too, is not the reason for his eminence. For even if nobody cares for him, he is still a human being."

■ ■ ■

Rodney informed me of a couple of items before Mass on Sunday. First, the approaching Labor Day weekend could be a problem, since there were going to be many suspicious strangers in town. Rodney was always preparing for the imminent appearance of "the Russians" in Portland. I told him that he was in control, so, hey, no sweat. Second, it was important that I know that a number of "submarine people"—his allies—were present at the Mass. This second piece of inside information no doubt added to his strange brand of perpetual consolation.

For Rodney, the Mass is a great pageant that offers fodder for his incredible imagination. Each moment and person, each grunt and groan, each transition point and prayer pause is shoehorned into his fantasy life.

Despite the fixed delusional system that interferes with Rodney's perception of reality, he maintains a certain kind of lucidity. He always manages to intensify the beauty and sanctity of the worship by his prayers for the world and for specific people in the world (a peacemaker, a sick woman, a country in need). He is amazing. I think he is an angel.

. . .

In the middle of Mass this evening, an intoxicated man wobble-walked right into the church, made a beeline for the altar, took a left-hand turn, and wound up on his knees in front of the statue of the Virgin Mary. He began yelling pious and incoherent remarks at the statue. I walked off the altar, identified myself, and asked him to be quiet, but he darted away, feinting to hit me.

"I don't care who you are!" he screamed.

I followed him, asking him to leave, and thought I had succeeded when a self-righteous guy butted in and took him into the pew, rebuking me indignantly for daring to kick anybody out of the church. I let it go, conscious of the rest of the congregation and hoping that things would settle down. As soon as he was in the pew, the drunk unleashed an unearthly noise, something between a groan and a bellow. I felt the hair on the back of my neck rise. At that point I asked him to leave, threatening to call the police. He stumbled out of the chapel, his defending buddy departing with him.

It shook me up. The ensuing Mass seemed artificial and wooden. I felt disconnected and troubled.

After Mass, as if to ensure that the preceding incident didn't reduce all life to something serious, I was approached by a young-looking Frederick, who enthusiastically talked to me about the skateboard tournament he had set up, which was scheduled to take place underneath the Burnside Bridge. He had purchased all the trophies, and by the way, would I mind being the judge? It was funny in the way sudden bizarre moments can be funny: here was this earnest skateboarder, seemingly oblivious to the incident with the intoxicated man that had occurred only a short while before.

I begged off the judging request. However much wisdom Frederick had attributed to me, the truth is that I know nothing about the meritorious intricacies of that sport, except to recognize the speed of some of its practitioners as they bear down on me, hell-bent, in the streets.

■ ■ ■

A woman who suffers from depression and convoluted delusions came up to me after Mass today. The first sign I had that she was in trouble were the skintight gloves she was wearing on such a warm day. Seems she had found out through "private" sources that I, as well as seven other people with whom I am friends, have AIDS. No more touching, please; indeed, she never wanted to talk to me again. I knew that she had a crush on me, so I guess this was her way of dealing with it. There was this all-knowing, leering smile on her face. It scared me. She is so sick; one does not know the direction in which her delusions might lead her.

■ ■ ■

At Mass today, Sandy induced one of her pseudoseizures. They always get people's attention. When I asked her if she wanted some help, she turned on me like a cannon and started screaming at me. I am not sure what is happening during these episodes. I called the paramedics, who screeched their way right up to the front door of the chapel. They convinced her to go to the hospital, which is what she wanted. I thought to myself as they were wheeling her out that she can be repulsive, out of hinge with my orderly way of doing things.

The joke is on me. *There isn't order down here, Gary; you are living and working with people who do not see it your way.* In these moments, I usually end up staring into the paradox of God's love: that the greatest in the kingdom of God are the least of my brothers and sisters.

■ ■ ■

Between the two Sunday morning Masses yesterday at the Downtown Chapel, I facilitated a discussion on the Gospel passage for the day. These discussions are held every Sunday and are attended faithfully by a core of about a dozen people plus some occasional visitors.

Most of the attendees at these meetings are residents of Old Town. They are educated and uneducated, mentally ill and mentally healthy, poor and middle class. I could introduce them to a theology professor as experts in this field. Each one is uniquely equipped for the task of breaking open the Gospel. Today, there was Frank, just out of prison, a Native American man with a special understanding of the sacred; Eunice, who suffered from delusions and depression but sympathized with the people of the New Testament; Pauline, who giggled a lot and who possessed nothing but optimistic and warm insights about the particular Scripture reading; Paul, disarmingly earnest, bearing a dozen two-day-old doughnuts for the Gospel busters; Doreen, a retired nurse who clearly had spent a lifetime meditating on the person of Christ. There was another individual present, whom I called Silent Bob. He sat across from me, for the most part never saying anything, his scraggly-haired head buried in his chest. But when there was an enthusiastic, and therefore splendid, explanation of Scripture, he would raise his head, look at me, and smile and nod, as if to say, "Now *that* was one helluva insight."

Those Sunday morning conversations amaze me. They start out with everyone talking at once, each person expressing a different idea. Momentarily the discussion threatens to fall apart. Inevitably it comes together. The truth of it all emerges in the unaffected determination and transparent searching of individuals sifting through the Gospel. They reveal the heart of liberation theology, which is that the poor advance to the truth of the Gospel, are empowered by it, and become architects of their own liberation.

■ ■ ■

I celebrated Mass recently at one of the Portland churches, only a few miles from my world down here but light years away in terms of people and concerns. But preaching the Gospel is a function of trying to reach the human heart, whether people are poor or rich or middle class. And the bad breaks and tragic mysteries of life exist in plenitude in a city parish.

I remember Pamela at that Mass, a wonderful young woman, seated in her wheelchair in front of the congregation, literally twisted in her cerebral palsy. When I went to her during the time when the congregation was exchanging a gesture of peace, she clung to me, her hands grasping mine, her head pressed to my head. Later, in front of the church, she tried to tell me something as saliva dribbled down her smiling, glad-to-see-me face. I could not understand her. Helplessly, I looked to her father for a translation, and he repeated his daughter's unforgettable words: "I wish I could talk to you."

How she longed to communicate, to be able to look another human being in the face and say "hello" or "thank you" or "it is nice to talk with you" without her effort being an excruciating summons to every screwed-up nerve and synapse in her body and brain. How she would have given anything for five minutes in which to say to me, to her parents, to anyone, "I love you" or "How about that barn-burner game we saw last night" or "I hurt" or "Could you hold me, say, for about twenty-four hours?" It is incomprehensible, this handicap.

Ah, Pamela, what am I to do? How can I ever get into your world, how can you ever get out, and does the whole bleeping thing make you want to scream to God, "Why?"

The methods of the Divine are utterly lost on me when I am in the presence of a Pamela. And my words sound so empty. I can say, "Well, God loves you," and I have said that, but it sounds so wooden in the face of certain kinds of suffering. If I were someone like Pamela and some priest uttered those words to me, I'd throw rotten eggs at him. People want to run on good legs and eat with ease when they are hungry and drink carelessly when they are thirsty and make love with their beloved; they want to be able, in short, to see and feel and touch and live a long life. They don't want my pious platitudes when they have been robbed of these things. If I am to offer any comfort to them, I must find another part of my heart, the part that communicates my desire to walk with them. There is wisdom there, and humility, and a key to my own selfish heart and my delusions of personal indestructibility. It seems to me, if I am honest, that, as St. Paul said, "it is when I am weak that I am strong" (2 Corinthians 12:10).

It probably means so little to people who suffer for me to say, "You have the secret to who I am." It is probably best for me to shut up and walk with them in silence.

■ ■ ■

Tonight, at the Holy Thursday liturgy, many of the poor were present, having their feet gently washed and dried by others in imitation of Jesus. When I saw it all in front of me—the poor, the washing basins, the awkwardness of the washers, the faces of the silent and reverent congregation—I realized once again what the sanctity of service is and that the truth of the heart of Christ is found in the washing of feet. When I have washed feet, I have realized that it is only from below that I can really see what is above.

A long time ago I read a reflection by Luigi Santucci in his book *Meeting Jesus* about the bowl that Christ used in washing the feet of his disciples. I remember thinking, like him, that if I had to choose some relic of the Passion, I wouldn't pick up a scourge or a spear, but that round bowl of dirty water. And I would want to go around the world with that receptacle under my arm, looking only at people's feet; and for each one I'd tie a towel around me, bend down, and never raise my eyes higher than their ankles, so as not to distinguish friends from enemies. I'd wash the feet of atheists, drug addicts, arms dealers, murderers, pimps, abusers of all kinds—and all in silence, until they understood.

Before retiring for the night, the sights and sounds of the liturgy still ringing through me, I heard on the radio an interview with a Memphis pastor who had been with Martin Luther King Jr. at the motel where the civil rights leader was assassinated. Over the years this same pastor had reflected on the meaning of it all and was led to believe that he was called to be a witness to Dr. King's life and death.

That is partly how I feel about my life. I am a witness to a movement in me that I can't understand or articulate. As impossible as it is for me to understand my call to service, there will be people who do get it and who can point to me and say, "There it is, there is faith in operation, there is a believer, there is the holy operating in another human being. It is the guy with the bowl of dirty water in his hands." They will recognize what they know to be the living presence of the heart of God. I am a witness to that heart, and this may, in the end, be my only contribution, homely and undramatic as it is. I am like the spectacular yet fleeting blooming of an Arizona cactus plant: for just a few days, the world is full of a new and astonishing color.

There are times on the streets when I wonder what the hell I am doing. And there are moments, usually humdrum and unspectacular, during which I realize that I am to bloom for just a few days so that I might give glory in my work to another kind of beauty that works in and through me. I rebel against this kind of divine interference in my life, especially when it conflicts with my other great loves. But Jeremiah makes it clear that no one chooses to fall into the hands of the living God.

> *You have seduced me, Yahweh, and I have let myself*
> *be seduced;*
> *you have overpowered me: you were the stronger. . . .*
> *I used to say, "I will not think about him,*
> *I will not speak in his name any more."*
> *Then there seemed to be a fire burning in my heart,*
> *imprisoned in my bones.*
> *The effort to restrain it wearied me,*
> *I could not bear it.*
>
> JEREMIAH 20:7, 9

No one in the service of the poor, who is honest, pats himself or herself on the back. If he or she does, it is not for long. I realize that God brought me into this world, blessed with skills and talents. The only thing that makes sense to me is to use them in the service of the poor. It is at their feet that I find myself.

chapter nine

JAILHOUSE PRAYERS:

LEARNING TO TRUST BEHIND BARS

The imprisoned are the poorest of the poor.

My stomach cramps up each time I walk into the local county jail. It is a hard place for the soul, for many reasons: the somber gray-white walls, the electric doors that clang open and snap shut behind me as though expressing anger over my presence, the silent cameras that watch over every nook and cranny in the building, the sterile smell of indifference, the severe faces of most of the inmates and correction officers.

I am at least comforted by the fact that I can start out my time at the jail by checking in with the jail chaplain, a warm and direct Baptist minister who has been there for years and is my top resource for the daunting tasks of understanding specific inmate problems and crafting the art of ministry in jail. Chaplain Lewis owns that rare heart that copes day after day with people who do time, and he knows how to tiptoe through the minefields of correction politics.

Sometimes the church, out of its duty to advocate for the poor who are incarcerated, must take stands that run at right angles to the methods of the state, whether it is fighting for proper diets or challenging abusive policies. Chaplain Lewis is on the front line of these battles.

In the office I pick up messages from inmates who have requested to see a Catholic priest. From there I proceed to the modules that house the inmates. On some floors it is so crowded that the men must double-bunk in one of the thirty cells in a module.

■ ■ ■

Yesterday at the jail I met with Toby, a thirty-five-year-old man who wanted to share Bible reflections. He has a history of assault.

I asked a few questions about his background. On occasion, family history leaves me interiorly shaking my head: the innocence and genuine interest of my questions stand in contrast to the enormity of the responses.

"Mom and dad?"

"Both dead," he said. "My mom overdosed herself on sleeping pills; Dad was shot to death. My brother is in San Quentin doing two life terms plus a day; he'll be in there until he dies. He murdered two guys back in 1979."

"Ever done time before?"

"Yes, one stretch for nine years. I was with my brother then. This time I assaulted someone for pulling a knife on me. Actually, I was the one who shot and killed my father. I caught him raping my sister."

And so it went. Toby is a good man, decent, friendly. There was nothing apathetic about him or about what he said, and his whole story was sprinkled with smiles and fleeting tears. Although his background has clearly had an effect on him, it seems that such a life would have embittered—indeed, destroyed—many other men.

Our lives become so caught up in the unresolved, painful experiences of our younger years: we either face them head-on, sometimes with sudden catastrophic results, or they linger, like a latent virus, and emerge periodically, debilitating our hunt for wholeness. On the other hand, it is a tribute to the human spirit—and I see this often in jail—that the very stuff that can destroy a person becomes the raw material for reclaiming the potential of one's life.

■ ■ ■

One day, as I was making my way through a module that housed sex offenders, a man, Don, crossed the concrete floor to where I was concluding a conversation with another inmate and asked if he could see me. He was a good-looking man with neatly cut hair; had he been walking past me on the streets, I would have guessed him to be a schoolteacher or a bank executive. He had a young face, but his eyes were older: forty, going on a hundred.

Don looked at me and plunged into weeping. He wept or was on the verge of tears for our entire first encounter.

"I've never been in jail, Father. I don't belong in here with the rest of these guys. I'm scared and alone and my family is in a state of shock. I know that it would be better for me to be out on bail and go through all this legal stuff while I am on the outside. I think I will go crazy if I remain in that cell every night and every day."

A few days earlier, Don had been arrested for pedophilia. He was a successful businessman, a suburbs kind of guy with all the trappings: a young wife, a couple of kids, barbecues for the neighborhood association, involvement in the PTA. In a flash, in one of those moments that change one's life forever, he went from the good and respected superguy to a menacing outcast. But as aware as I was that his world was crumbling, I was more aware of the little people he had harmed—harmed so much that their lives would always bear a psychic fault line created by his seductions.

Ours was one of those conversations that are always difficult for me. I am confronted with and eventually impaled on that double-edged sword to which prison chaplains must expose themselves. On the one hand, I feel grief over a pained and remorseful inmate who is working through the tragic and mind-numbing consequences of his or her behavior, and on the other hand, I feel disgust and sadness over a crime that was inflicted on innocent victims—in this case, vulnerable, defenseless children.

Given the nature of his crime, there was no way that Don would be released on bail. He did not go crazy, but he became very depressed. For months, as the machinery of prosecution slowly ground out facts, woe, and heartache, I saw Don once a week. We visited. We prayed. For a long time he whistled in the dark, living in denial in the worst way. No matter how many times I brought up the horror story in which he had been the monster, and no matter how often I tried to point out the system's severity with people convicted of a crime such as his, he just didn't get it. And he was a very intelligent man.

Slowly, as family and friends hammered him with the truth (indeed, some of them even pulled away in despair), and when it became clear that the state would punish him, he began to accept the grim revelation of his sickness and how it had turned his life into a nightmare. He gained the insight that every recovering addict has.

The judge gave him the maximum sentence and sent him to a facility that will offer him the psychiatric help he needs. He will not leave prison until he is an old man. He will be forever separated from family members who—understandably—have terminated their relationships with him.

After the sentencing, I spoke with him briefly, then slowly walked home, wrapped up in my own thoughts as well as the nippy morning fog. I was very sad—sad for all the lives that had been betrayed and wounded by his lived lie. I prayed for him, for his family, for his friends, and for the injured children.

I had to dig down to my deepest beliefs, because in vulnerable moments like this, the entire tragedy leaves me staring at the absurd. I believe that God continues to love us regardless of who we are and what we do. But I know, too, that God's unwavering love also gives us freedom, and that freedom comes with responsibility. Neither Don nor I nor anyone who falls on his or her face in worship of God can be discharged from the task of acting responsibly.

God's love will work with Don as he confronts his sickness, makes responsible choices, and turns to God for the grace, protection, and guidance that will be the foundation for his choices. May he become a free man. May he become a man of surrender.

■ ■ ■

Jails, more and more, have become warehouses for people with mental illness. The stats sum it up: of the almost two million jail and prison inmates in the United States, almost three hundred thousand are people with serious mental illness. Twenty percent of these mentally ill inmates were homeless when they were incarcerated. Seventy-five percent of the incarcerated mentally ill have been arrested before. They are more likely than inmates who are not mentally ill to break the rules, so they frequently wind up having time added to their sentence.

I arrived at the jail one day and picked up a request from Michael, who was locked in isolation at the justice center jail. He wanted to make a confession. Isolation cells on this floor, referred to as the hole, are monitored closely. The emphasis here is on maximum security.

Michael suffers from mental illness. He has cycled in and out of jail for years and is a troublemaker even when on antipsychotic medication.

I wound up talking to him from the central control office of the isolation cells by means of an intercom. He was locked away and could not have face-to-face visits, even with an experienced chaplain like me. He communicated in the high-speed, pressured speech of the schizophrenic. I had a difficult time trying to sort out his issues without seeing him, especially because I was conscious of the security officer standing next to me, monitoring all the cells. There was another inmate near Mike's cell, and I could hear him yelling in the background. Finally Michael screamed, "Shut up, you stupid motherfucker, I'm talking to a Father!" All became quiet momentarily, and he made his rambling point.

In situations like this, it is controlled chaos. I wish I had the code to unlock Michael's mind. But no such code exists. All I can bring to the conversation are my heart and my trust that God wants me in the midst of this chaos. The imprisoned are the poorest of the poor. If the heart of God is to be found anywhere, it is to be found in the hole.

■ ■ ■

I had a sad talk with twenty-eight-year-old Brian at the jail today. He was alternately angry and grief stricken. His arrest had separated him from his four children, and now they were with their mother. She and Brian are divorced and hate each other. He was looking at a rape charge, which he claimed was all trumped up by a persuasive prostitute who was trying to rip him off.

There he was, clearly a fragile guy, looking at five years, if he copped a plea, or twenty years, if he chose to go on trial and was convicted. He was frantic and furious, his desperate situation pouring over him like lava. He wept in the crowded module and kept saying through his tears, "I did not do it, I did not do it." He is half-crazed in the absence of his daughters, and he knows that his chances of seeing them in the near future are not good. After we talked, I prayed with him, my hand of blessing resting momentarily on his arm.

■ ■ ■

Another heartbreaker. A twenty-one-year-old Mexican national was in jail for possession of drugs with the intent to sell, and the authorities informed him last night that his older brother, who was twenty-four, had overdosed on cocaine and died in a Portland apartment. Domingo spoke no English and refused to give any kind of address or phone number for his family in Mexico City. The police and county needed this information in order to resolve the disposition of his brother's remains. He asked to speak with a priest. Because he trusted me, I was able to get the information.

What could be more ravaging to the human spirit? Here Domingo was, alone in a jail, with no chance to mourn over the body of his brother, no chance to grieve with his family, and looking at some considerable jail time. And a long way from home.

■ ■ ■

Today was a blitz day in the jail, and I am whipped from moving through the turmoil and disarray that characterize the lives of many in prison.

Down in the hole I visited Marty, an intelligent man facing a mountain of charges related to his transmission of drugs. The feds got him on possession of the worst kind, and they had threatened him not only with forty years but also with the confiscation of all his property. It was his first time in jail. He had a family and, according to him, was a successful businessman. He needed someone to talk to, but given the nature of security in that particular part of the jail, we had to talk through a slot in the wall of isolation's central command office.

The slot we spoke through was like a mail slot. I was leaning forward in a chair, and he was on his knees on the other side of the wall. At different times I would see his eyes, his eyebrows, his mouth, his chin, and tears on his cheeks. He was desperate, thinking of suicide and, of course, denying the crime. "A terrible misunderstanding," he said.

Behind me, an officer went about his business, attempting not to hear anything (though they hear everything). Before I left, Marty and I prayed through the mail slot.

Later on I met with Wyatt, a handsome twenty-eight year old who was in on yet another burglary charge. His parents were killed in a plane crash when he was twelve, perhaps half a dozen years prior to the onset of his schizophrenia, and his older brother—his only sibling—overdosed on heroin five years ago in a ratty old SRO. Throw in his drug addiction and a severe attention deficit disorder, and his is a gloomy prognosis. He could be looking at years of incarceration unless the system can help him. It certainly won't by repeatedly locking him up. He lives in fear that he will be sent to the state penitentiary; he smiled disconnectedly at that prospect and then described his game plan should he be asked to "perform" in the Salem facility. He was repeatedly raped as a youth in juvenile detention. He expects no less at the big house.

After our colloquy, Wyatt asked if we could pray. To be around him when he prays is humbling. His prayer always goes something like this: "Lord God, I pray first of all for the brothers and sisters in this jail, that you might strengthen them. I pray for the people who come to the Downtown Chapel to get something to eat and for the staff that provides for them; I pray for all the poor; I pray in thanksgiving for all the people who help me here and for Father Gary, who comes to see me. Please watch over him and his work. I pray for myself that I might get better."

He is a wonderful human being who has done some bad things. But they are so pathetically petty next to his need for long-term care. His problems have been unceasing, almost from birth. He is alone. Terribly, unyieldingly alone. He has never possessed the social skills to develop those friendships and love relationships that we all take for granted and need for the deep and healthy part of us to grow. Such relationships are, quite frankly, the difference between life and death. When I think of the thousands of people stuck on themselves, living a life of self-indulgence and yet potentially able to spend time visiting and being a friend to people like Wyatt, I become very sad and frustrated.

■ ■ ■

I was walking out of the chapel today, on my way to jail, when I heard my name. And there was James, recently out of a Colorado penitentiary. He had aged in two years but had retained his infectious smile, which emerged beneath those squinty eyes, surrounded by crow's-feet. Later that day, we chatted over lunch. He is the consummate extrovert, and he spent an hour regaling me with tales about his days on the road, traveling through Utah, Montana, Washington, and Oregon. He did a lot of thinking; smoked too many rolled cigarettes; got laid a few times; lost his pet bird, Harv (short for Harvard). Presently he is residing in southern Oregon, but he had a chance to come up and see me. The man was clean and sober.

It was an interesting scene: the priest and the ex-convict chatting in a booth at Burger King. I reflected, as we shared our lives once again, that James was a unique man, his own kind of flower in this universe, trouble and all, giving his own kind of glory to God. He is fiercely loyal to our friendship. To connect with him again was a gentle affirmation of this ministry, in which I try to be a person of love, putting flesh on faith. It revealed how this ministry of presence extends through time and space: on the streets in another city ten years ago, through humdrum prison correspondence, by means of the occasional long-distance phone call, and now over coffee and a Whopper in Portland. And, of course, through all the thoughts and prayers we've had for each other through the years.

Care for James, Holy God. Watch over him, travel with him, and by your love bring him to the truth of who he is to be. Keep us in each other's lives.

■ ■ ■

George was tall and had prematurely gray hair. I thought that if he were in a suit instead of the obligatory blue jail-issued jumpsuit and brown sandals, he could pass for a CEO on the front of *GQ.*

He came up to me as soon as I walked into the module of the justice center jail. We had met only once on the outside; I was an acquaintance of his girlfriend, and she had introduced me to him one day at a bus stop.

Unbelievably, he had killed some guy in a bar. He had thrust a knife into the heart of another man.

His was one of those pathetically sad stories of the alcoholic world. George had been sober for a year and decided to have a celebratory drink. One drink led to the next, and before long, George, intoxicated, got into a machismo-fueled altercation with another drunk. He didn't even know the man, who was no sweetheart himself, having a history of felonies involving drug trafficking. But whatever the checkered history of the other man, George had killed him. After his arrest he learned that he could be looking at anything from diminished manslaughter to murder.

He went through the whole story with me. He was sorry that he had killed the man. He was in danger because the deceased had friends in the jail, so he had to constantly watch his back. He said the killing was in self-defense, since the man had a gun.

Inconveniently for George, the dead man's friends hid the weapon before the police arrived. George was in a state of shock. His life had been so promising after years of messing around: he had a solid job as a retailer, a girlfriend, sobriety.

As the weeks went by, George, like some kind of Job, was visited by more grief and setbacks. The prosecutors decided to charge him with murder, a conviction that entailed ten to fifteen years. On top of that, his girlfriend, a key to contacting witnesses for him on the outside, started drinking heavily. Then she split up with him over the phone.

He sat there, his eyes full of tears, describing the emptiness of it all. He cried so much that he stopped using handkerchiefs and started using a huge towel, which he draped around his neck. As I talked with him and listened to him weep, I recalled past moments of grief when my world had crashed and how terrible I had felt. I remembered how I found, in my friends, sustaining courage to push on in the darkness: friends who sat with me, walked and talked with me—indeed, rocked me in their arms when words seemed empty and meaningless. No one can be present to grief unless he or she has been there. And no pious remarks will defang grief. Only another human being who has experienced suffering in his or her own bones can presume to walk with the hurting man or woman. So I tried to be present to this man's overpowering hurt, knowing that in time he would get through the darkness, but, for the short term, he needed the best kind of selfless support.

Two months later, during another jail visit, George told me that he had learned through a cousin that his girlfriend had tested positive for HIV. He speculated, almost cynically, that this was a result of her screwing around after he had entered the slammer. Severe alcoholism and HIV: now there is the ultimate deadly combination. Oddly enough, like someone who has been beaten down by events, George was amazingly unmoved by the news. Maybe it was the gone-numb syndrome. In the meantime he had tested negative for HIV. I told him that he was lucky, because she had to have had it when they were together, given the short time that they had been separated.

When the trial came, he didn't have a chance. He was up against an abundance of prosecution witnesses and a particularly aggressive prosecutor who, incidentally, frown-faced me every time I appeared in the gallery, especially if I was in clerical clothes. I think he thought I was prejudicing the jury ("How can this be a bad man if he has a priest as a friend?"). Why do I always get the feeling that some prosecutors who deal with the poor are climbers, seeing the Georges of this world as fresh meat?

It is always painful for me, as it is for most prison chaplains, to see a man or a woman attacked so directly in the courtroom, all in an effort to pile as many collateral accusations on the defendant as possible, the implication being that he or she is intrinsically evil. It is difficult because we have come to know and love the person, perhaps having seen him or her turn dark places in his or her heart into light. There would not be time to consider the possibility that this man did kill in self-defense, to explain that I had seen his tears and had been around the streets long enough to know that he might possibly be speaking the truth. Nope, said the prosecutor, he was a murderer and that was all there was to it.

His lawyer, the county's hired gun, seemed to have more important things to do and appeared befuddled by just about everything. At the last minute, desperate, he actually subpoenaed me. Of course, anything I could say about George would be hearsay and therefore would not be applicable in court. I understand this and know that it is, ultimately, for the victim's protection, but it still left me wondering how the criminal justice system ever gets to the heart of the criminal. I suppose that is not its task. That is the task of the priest.

George received ten years with no parole.

We embraced for the last time as he was being taken out. "Thanks, Father," he told me. "You have been more than a friend. I will pray for you." We stay in touch by writing.

■ ■ ■

It was a busy day at the jail, one rich in human contact, in the power of the sacrament of reconciliation, and in people endeavoring to make their peace with God. Mike made a confession for the first time in fifteen years. He is a huge man, has a shaved head, and looks like he could eat nails for breakfast. But oh so gentle. He will probably spend a lot of time in a federal prison.

We talked about so many things outside the context of the confession: his use of crack (his "drug of choice"), relentless and always available sex ("I have used women"), his life of ripping and robbing ("The only people I didn't hit or steal from were my mom and dad"). There are signs now of change, of him wanting to do something positive in his life. He has come to terms with his fear of alienating the old gang of thugs that he used to run with, people who have contacts in the prison system. His old girlfriend is into Satanism and heroin, which brings sadness into his face, but he knows he must move on.

After years in jail and prison ministry, I still don't know for certain when I am looking at a "jailhouse conversion" or the real deal of spiritual metamorphosis. But more and more, as I meet and come to know individuals in the jails, I trust my instincts. In Mike's case, because he is older, I perceive a kind of benevolent weariness of self. I always take younger guys who are suddenly into religion with a grain of salt, even as I am hopeful. I say hopeful because they wouldn't be talking to me if something wasn't going on inside of them. They don't seek me out for a jail favor; I have no pull in the system.

The older guys have a wisdom that is born not of desperation but of an acceptance of their status and an unwillingness to continue to con themselves. There is a point in one's self-realized poverty where humility and truth make their entry. Power and its little brothers, honor and reputation, are the agenda of the young. This agenda blinds them and closes them off to change, to their very hearts' longings. But it is bullshit for one like Mike, who is seeking out answers to very existential questions: Where is my heart? Where do I want to go with my heart?

Enter the Holy Spirit.

Help him, O God, and let not the hunt for truth be swallowed up in all the chaos and loneliness of incarceration.

■ ■ ■

These moments at the jail are sobering journeys into human hearts, through electric doors and the barriers produced by human pain. Jail is a place where a word can land you in isolation, where a sucker punch can be right around the corner, where grinding loneliness and only momentary flashes of hope exist, and where bitterness about life is worn like a tattoo. For me, ministering in jail is an experience in head-shaking acceptance, which is to say that I am in the presence of brothers and sisters who have made some awful decisions that have affected and will continue to affect them and their loved ones—in some cases, for good, for life, forever. The stories I hear come at me like a posse riding over a ridge: stories of alcoholism's disasters, spousal abuse, threats, murder, kidnapping, illegal immigration, burglary, statutory rape, bank robbery, drug dealing, theft, car jacking, assault, prostitution, drunk driving, pedophilia.

And yet, I think the biggest story is that an incarcerated human being would want to unburden his or her heart with the kind of trust that one would think had deserted this part of the universe.

chapter ten

POVERTY IS NOT A CRIME:

EDDIE'S LETTER

It's sometimes cold outside, but not as cold as
people.

Not too long ago, I heard a
radio talk-show host attack street people and all who sit on our
streets with outstretched hands and hats hoping to solicit a few
bucks. With the ivory-tower perspective of the well-heeled (and
within the safety of his studio), he wrote off those of our society
who are possessed by the demons of booze and drugs and mental
illness and poverty and bad luck. He was a chip off the cultural
block, sharing the mind-set of a culture that has declared war on
the homeless poor, a war in which our cities try to regulate beg-
gars and edge poor people out of existence. Out of sight, out of
mind. From this shock jock's viewpoint, it is a crime to be poor
and homeless.

The moral crime is that people like this jerk have no interest in finding out anything about the human being who stands on the corner, smelling and hungry. Were he to meet one such person and hear that individual's story, he might understand the beating heart before him and the reasons why that luckless individual is standing there looking for a handout.

I've known Eddie for a long time. He wrote the following for me. It is a story that explains the struggles of the man and what makes up his heart. It is a poignant response to those who so blithely dismiss the homeless.

My name is Eddie. I have a disability. It's Depression and Paranoia. As a little boy I was beat and punished for wetting the bed. I think I was three or four years old. When my sister and I went to live with my aunt, I think that's when Paranoia/Depression came into my life. My sister would have to clean up the whole house and I would have to go to work in the cotton fields with my aunt. She said we would have to work for our room and board. I had a bed-wetting problem, to where I ruined the bed. She and my cousin would beat me with a stick/cord/belt across my back, legs, and buttocks. After the beatings she would punish me by making me kneel on the concrete floor all day without moving from that position. She would also punish me other ways. Once she put a live frog down my pants. She said I would have to keep it there all day. I jumped up and down and ran around, thinking the frog was going to eat me alive. I started screaming and crying. I ran to the bathroom and I threw the frog out the window. My cousin ran behind me and thought I threw the frog down the toilet and flushed it. So he grabbed me by the hair and pushed my head down the toilet and flushed it several times. I struggled for air and I must have hit him, because the next day I woke up in the closet with bruises on me. My sister was crying, saying, "I will get us out of here someday."

One time my aunt made one of my cousins pee in a glass and I was to drink it or get a beating and have to kneel on the concrete floor. I didn't want to kneel on the concrete floor because my knees were bleeding from kneeling so long. So I drank it.

One time I had to use the bathroom and I was too far from the house and I shit in my pants. When I got home, my aunt made me take a bath, but before I was to eat it or get a beating. I put it in my mouth and tasted it. I don't think I ate it. I woke up in the closet again with bruises.

One time my aunt made me dress in girls' clothes and sent me outside where everyone could see me. I was so embarrassed that day.

Another time my aunt called me from the playground where I usually played by myself. I ran home because I didn't want to upset my aunt or she would either pinch me or slap me. I didn't know she had cut the cord to the plug of the washing machine. There was a puddle of water on the ground. She also had an audience of people in her room, so I plugged in the plug to the socket and it shocked the life out of me. It threw me about five feet away. They all started laughing at me. All I could do was cry.

One time when I was getting a beating my sister said she would do anything if they would stop beating me. One time someone told me to go out and play and when I snuck up to the back door and I looked inside, someone was molesting my sister. I didn't do or say anything.

One time my aunt made me sit on the toilet all night long. My sister and I finally ran away from there to my dad's. At fifteen years old my dad put me to work for him on the fishing boat because I was having troubles at school. [It was that] or go to reform school for bad boys. I cried because no one knew I had a disability or sent me to a doctor. I cried some more. I swallowed my hopes and dreams. My dad asked me why I was withdrawing from everyone and I told him the story and he said I was lying so I was treated like an outsider. I always was trying to be the best that I could for everyone but never amounting to shit. At thirteen years old I was drinking with a man, a wino who would buy my beers for me. At eighteen years old I was a full-blown alcoholic. When I turned twenty years old I left my dad's home. Before I left, my stepmother asked me why do you have to leave. I said I was going to find myself. I didn't go looking for myself. I went to find something more precious than that. I was looking for my spirit that someone stole. I was getting into trouble with the law from the time I was twenty to the time I was forty-five. I also lived on the streets for twenty years. With no education and no skills I first had to sell myself or sell drugs to make it on the streets. No one gives you shit or gives a shit about you.

But I'm off the streets for now. But I know there are others out there like me with mental problems and maybe doing the same things I did. I would love to help them so they don't have to go through what I did and so they can have a better life. May God bless them.

Sometimes it's hard living on the streets. And there are some people that don't understand homelessness. Some of them get treated like shit. It's sometimes cold outside, but not as cold as people. I am now recovering from alcoholism and drug addiction. But I don't know if I'll ever recover from physical and mental abuse. I've also been afraid of making a family, because I don't know how I would act or react.

Stop the abuse! You're killing God's children spiritually.

Eddie

P.S. If you ever look into a homeless person's eyes, don't judge them. Simply say something nice. I haven't seen my sister for over twenty-five years. I wish I could see her again.

After all this, incredibly, Eddie has survived. His plea serves as an invitation to those of us who want to understand and as a condemnation of those fools who write off the homeless as losers who brought their troubles upon themselves.

chapter eleven

THE LEPER:

ROBERT'S STORY

We were the apple and the orange, united and
bound by the searching love of our mutual Creator.

Today, with a partner from the Macdonald Center, I made my first visit to Robert, a sick young man who lives in a hotel just off Burnside. His name had been given to us by a health care professional who thought he might like a visit.

Robert is a frail man of thirty-eight, balding prematurely. In a disarming burst of candor, he admitted to being manic-depressive, homosexual, drug addicted, and HIV positive. His seedy third-floor room was filthy and had a pervasive bad odor, clearly that of dead mice, that left me gagging for the first five minutes of our visit.

The walls were covered with posters of heavy-metal performers, some of his drawings, and years of wear and tear. In one corner of the room, where the wall and ceiling joined, a battalion of cock-roaches casually gathered around the hot-water pipe, like a herd of little black sheep who could walk upside down. They seemed to be grazing on paint chips from the peeling wall but made periodic excursions down to the food fields of Robert's floor or, in longer forays, to the top of his dilapidated TV (a good place to hide food from the mice). I had never seen roaches move so slowly.

Robert was a little high, and I got the feeling that drugs enabled him to move outside the depressive elements of his life, converse, and relate. He appreciated the opportunity to talk, and after our visit he followed us out into the hallway, where he shook our hands and then gave both of us an embrace.

Alone in a Skid Row hotel, in a hot, smelly room. Alone, feeling bad about himself. I thought while we were chatting that he must cry a lot; I sensed simultaneously in him an off-the-charts interior pain and an enormous reservoir of sensitivity.

June 30, Wednesday

Today was my fourth visit with Robert. He had been drinking beer but had not dropped off into depression. He is slowly revealing the details of his life: years of wandering, sleeping in the streets, sexual promiscuity, several attempted suicides. He now has a crush on me, but it has become clear to him that however suggestive he might be, I simply am not on that planet when it comes to the reasons why I entered his life.

I felt that if we got past all his usual ways of relating to men (flirting, drugs, sex, adios) he might begin to discover the part of his heart that had gone into hiding when he was a young man. All of his sexual behavior is an entity, disconnected from the heart of the man himself. Some of his behavior leaves me disgusted, and I have to fight through my feelings in order to meet him on a level that communicates care. I know that his behavior is a manifestation of a ruthless sickness that was inflicted on him and that he continues to inflict on himself. It is as though he grew up in a closet and never came out of the darkness.

August 16, Monday

I had not seen Robert for several weeks, partly because he decided he did not want to see me. Then today he showed up at the Outreach office and asked if we could connect again. He had just left the hospital after a bout with pneumonia. He is now heading into full-blown AIDS. His immune system has broken down, and opportunistic diseases are ransacking his entire body in the hunt for what is vulnerable. They are busy about their business like the roaches that methodically raid Robert's room for food.

I was glad that he came in; it was clearly an overture to bring me into this part of his journey. His expression was a mix of shyness and fear. But I am seeing glimpses now of his heart.

God, give me the wisdom and courage to be with this man if he chooses to take me along. His pain is my pain.

November 17, Wednesday

Mary Sue and I made it through the cold and rainy streets to see Robert. He was feeling well. He has had some relief from his multiple physical problems, thanks to medication. He has backed off on the cocaine and is no longer involved in the madness of his out-of-control promiscuity. Many of the people from his past have died from AIDS.

Before we left, he suddenly asked if we would pray with him, and so we sat in that crappy little room, hand in hand, Mary Sue and Robert seated on his bed and me in a chair facing them. We lit the place up. It was a positive visit. It is clear that he trusts the two of us.

February 24, Thursday

I saw Robert at Good Samaritan Hospital today. He was out of it, and during my short visit he left his bed three times to dry heave in the bathroom. As usual, he was apologetic for "putting you through this, Father Gary." He is losing weight very quickly. He told me that he might consider going to an AIDS hospice after he leaves the hospital. I nodded in approval, but I was thinking that the administrative control necessary in such a place might be more than his independent self could stomach.

We prayed at the end of our visit. He is scared of death, conscious of the shambles that he thinks he has made of his life and of all the people he has injured. Could God ever forgive him? he constantly asks me. The God talk, I realize, has become more and more a part of his vocabulary.

June 20, Monday

Robert gave me a belated birthday gift today: an ocarina, a small musical instrument made of clay that sounds like a Peruvian pipe instrument when it is played. I was surprised; he's partially out of commission due to AIDS, yet he was able to track down a gift for me, and a unique one at that. His generosity and appreciation are emerging like a plant from a long-dormant bulb.

He has meningitis, another opportunistic disease, and the virus continues to kill his T cells. He is trusting more and more, and I sense that his trust has opened up everyone from the Macdonald Center who visits him regularly—Mary Sue, Mara, Joe, and myself. Now we are moving at him with all our wits and prayers.

Be with him, O God. Be his strength.

July 20, Wednesday

Robert has gone to Our House, an AIDS hospice. He seems very happy there and continues to manifest a steady change of attitude.

At this very moment, I am looking at an advance directive, a document that states that Robert has chosen me to make medical decisions for him when he is unable to make them for himself. This is a humbling experience, and I am moved by the trust that he is investing in me. If he can't make the final choice of life or death, he wants me to make it, just as surely as we all want our family or best friend to be involved in such a decision.

Looking around at the men at Our House, one gets a glimpse of what a terrible disease they are facing. It renders its victims' bodies vulnerable to disease and their souls vulnerable to despair. I am glad that Robert is among those who understand him and whom he understands. It is a community. What a strange paradox: Robert is finally part of a community of life, in which inevitable death is the linchpin.

August 8, Monday

Robert left the hospice over the weekend; I was called this morning by a member of the staff. After calling around, I found out that he was drinking and using cocaine again. It will destroy his chances of getting back into Our House. I should have figured that this sober period was too swift, too clean, too sure.

August 9, Tuesday

I caught up with Robert today as he was pushing his ripped-off Safeway cart to Esther's Pantry, a hole-in-the-wall that distributes food to people with HIV. It is located in one of the desolate warehouse sections not far from where he lives.

We talked as he rolled his cart back to his hotel. Yes, he did drink heavily on Sunday and slammed some coke. He did not want to talk, was depressed, and had a fuck-it-all attitude. Where now? He mentioned that he was going to see the doctor tomorrow. Given the unhealthy situation he has put himself in, his physical condition will take a turn for the worse. Nevertheless, I did not preach at him or whine about what he had abandoned. I just walked with him down the empty street. I asked him if he would be interested in going to the Oregon coast with me. Good move on my part. He had not been to the beach in years. Yes, he would like to go.

There we were, walking along that obscure street. What strange companions: Robert—short, street educated, gay, drug addicted, sexually promiscuous; and me—tall, university educated, straight, clean, and celibate. We were the apple and the orange, united and bound by the searching love of our mutual Creator.

September 3, Saturday

I drove Robert to the coast in the little Festiva that I have been using. We spent the day at the beach and had lunch at the Nestucca Sanctuary, a Jesuit retreat house on the coast. It was a good day. On arriving at the ocean, Robert must have stood and gazed at it for ten minutes before he could speak. "It is so beautiful, it is so beautiful," he kept repeating, as if he were looking at a new and wondrous color that had just come into existence. He said it had been fifteen years since he had been to the beach.

He could not get enough of the deer that hang around the Nestucca retreat facility. I thought that it would be a good place to take him sometime, for prayer and rest. He kept talking about coming back "to heal."

October 10, Thursday

Yesterday, when Mary Sue and I visited Robert, we caught him in a rampage of suicidal thinking. He had not gone for his radiation treatments and talked instead about another kind of destruction that was not so prolonged. The addict who is depressed is never far from taking himself out. I brought him a sand dollar from the beach, a sea urchin that is rich in Christian resurrection and life symbolism and an item that we had not been able to find on our previous trip. He wept over it, saying, "Damn you, you have screwed up my plans."

So he stayed alive one more day, buzzed and happy. I keep asking myself so many questions: *Will he kill himself? What is possible for God here? Can God cure him? Will God? And are such prayers pathetic? I mean, why keep him alive? For more loneliness, more empty sex, more pain, more despair, more mice, more cockroaches traveling across his face at night?*

November 11, Friday

Robert is in the hospital again. This time it is with infections caused by the use of dirty needles. The infection is in his leg and is working into his leg muscle. He already had an infection in one arm and apparently couldn't find a receptive vein in the other. So he moved on to the leg. I have known addicts who started shooting dope into their neck veins because all their arm and leg veins were used up.

I visited him today and took him smokes. Out of the serious discussion we had about the fact that he might lose his leg, we drifted into humorous reflections about a mutual acquaintance who had his leg amputated. Robert laughingly described times when he would draw faces on this guy's stump with markers.

February 4, Saturday

Robert's latest trip to the hospital, because of mysterious pains in his abdomen, was ominous in its conclusion: he was sent home amid some speculation that he has lymphoma. Mary Sue and I saw him in his SRO today after he returned. He was a little high on morphine, a drug his doctor has prescribed for him till the end. "Till the end"—now there is a gloomy expression. It is true that they are not doing anything for him except trying to keep him out of pain. If he has cancer, chemotherapy will do nothing for him, except totally deplete any resistance his body may have left.

I noticed Robert's cheekbones for the first time. They are sunken and extended. His is the gaunt face that I have seen on other AIDS patients, a sight that always makes me think of the survivors of the Nazi death camps.

The three of us talked about God's providence and how we have all been brought together. He asked me what *providence* meant. I explained, "It's like when you have some good friends and you would like them to meet each other so that they can grow and love in each other's presence; that is how God looks upon us and tries to enhance our lives."

May 31, Wednesday

Robert continues to waste away. So thin, yet present and gentle and not panicky. He is using less morphine.

Mara and I visited him today. He talked at length about belief and faith and God. "My resistance to God," he said, "has always been rooted in my feelings of being dirty. Like I am always a leper. But I know that we are all lepers to some degree and that in spite of that God still loves us. In fact, Jesus spent a lot of time with lepers, didn't he, Mara?"

He became silent. Then, with a look of peace that I had never seen on him, he said, "Father, can I ask you something?"

"Sure."

"Will you baptize me?"

So there it was, Robert asking to make the move; in many respects he had made the move long ago, but now he wanted to formalize it before the end of his life. He knows that he is dying, but what has been a revelation to him is that he is finding himself to be more and more at peace, and that he is loved. And he knows that he is not the author of that peace or that love. We decided to talk about the baptism soon and start the planning.

June 14, Wednesday

Mary Sue and I saw Robert today. He is in that dark room day after day, dying. He asked us questions, and we handled some immediately: yes, he would go to a hospice; yes, we would dispose of his ashes in the ocean. The baptism we will handle when his head is clear.

Then he surprised us with a statement that we will remember all of our lives. "I have something to ask of the two of you," he said.

Both of us were thinking, *What now? What terrible unresolved issue does he want us to deal with after he dies?*

He said, "Please continue to go out and be with other people like me, and love those people as you have loved me, and help them find meaning in their lives as you have done with me."

Of course we will, Robert. I placed my hand on his burning brow. It was my best gesture of assurance to a request that humbled me. Ah, such a request. I shall call it the Robert Project.

June 28, Wednesday

I baptized Robert today in a simple and modified baptismal liturgy. In attendance were the biggies of his life: Mary Sue, Sister Kate, Sister Cathy, Sister Elsie, a few friends, Mara and Joe (his chosen godparents), his favorite nurse at Good Sam, and assorted others. He came dressed in what he called "cat's ass" clothes, purchased by Sister Kate, who did a remarkable job, obtaining a pair of pants and a long-sleeved shirt that gave him a distinguished appearance in spite of his gaunt face and emaciated body. I told him he had a disco look.

I used the parable of the good Samaritan as a Gospel reading. I offered this commentary: "You are the good Samaritan, Robert, because you have pulled all of us out of the safe trenches of our lives. And your love—so squeezed out of you by life and history—you have claimed again and given back to us a hundredfold. What a grace it is to be present to see you commit your life to the one who is the author of your love. Your faith is healing oil for our wounds."

July 19, Wednesday

Tomorrow Robert will move to Our House, a hospice for AIDS patients. Today was his birthday; I picked up a couple of carnations, abundant in color, and Mary Sue brought him a chocolate milkshake. Though he was a bit groggy from his medication, he managed to chat for a while.

It was a time of gifts. He gave me a belated birthday present, a bluebird in stained glass. He gave us the gift of himself, that mysterious and direct persona that has invaded his life in the past several months.

He told us of the old man upstairs who stutters badly, who, his hand over his shy and quivering mouth, had come to say that he would miss Robert. Robert would have laughed in this fellow's face at one time not too long ago. He was very tired but sensed the pathos of the situation. He said, "Sit down, Gil," and he proceeded to grasp Gil's hand and console him. Robert told us, "However sick I am, this person's grief needed my attention. I told him: 'Listen, Gil, and I'll tell you a story of love you have never heard.'"

It was a haunting experience to leave Robert's room for the last time. As dismal and dreary as that room was, with its ancient odors of stale cigarettes and sick sex, with its discomfiting sights of cockroaches, darting mice, and crumbling posters—however bad all this was—the place was sacred for me. In that room, there were no obstacles to the grace of God or to the power of a human being to realize himself.

I saw you struggling in your blood as I was passing,
and I said to you as you lay in your blood: Live, and
grow like the grass of the fields.

Ezekiel 16:6–7

July 28, Friday

Robert is slipping. Last night Joe and Mara, like the great god-parents they are, spent the night with him. I saw him this afternoon. He was pretty out of it, very weak, and so emaciated that I ached. At one point, when he was finished in the bathroom, he asked me to come in to view his body, that bag of bones attached to his spinal column. His body was covered with blotches, caused by the Kaposi's sarcoma. It was as if some crazed tattoo artist had spilled his unconscious onto Robert's body in two tones: milky white and purple.

Later, as he lay there, my hand in his, he said, "Father Gary, there are some beautiful dolphins on your left cheek; now they have gone up your nose. Does your nose hurt?" At one point he reached over and touched my shoulder, leaving his hand there, and then said to me, "You are an angel."

Who is the angel here? Part of me hates the whole damn thing: his suffering, the premature death that is all around me, the smells and demands and commitment.

God, grant peace to him and to all of us, his family, who are part of his final passion.

July 31, Monday, the feast day of St. Ignatius, founder of the Jesuits

Sister Kate called me from Our House at two in the morning. Robert's breathing was very labored, and she doubted that he would survive the night. I went out right away.

When I arrived, his respiratory rate was extremely high and the body temperature in his extremities had lowered. He was dying.

I am sure he knew I was there; despite his diminished faculties, he could still respond to my touch. And so we held hands, beating back the fear and darkness with love. I asked St. Ignatius to intercede for him and that God might take him this day. "It's enough," I kept whispering to God.

Mara arrived for a brief period in the morning, after Kate had left. Michael, one of Robert's good friends, also came by. Mara and I left at eight o'clock after I placed a final kiss on Robert's clammy forehead. It would be the last time I would see him alive.

He died at 4:30. His godparents, Mara and Joe, were present. To the day I die, I will always understand his death, on that day—July 31, the feast day of St. Ignatius—as a sign for me.

I arrived back at the hospice at seven, after a long meeting with other Portland Jesuits. When I came around the corner of the hall, heading to his room, I could see that it was dark. Standing in the hallway were Mary Sue and Sister Kate. One look and I knew. I asked, "He's gone?" They nodded. I went into his room.

There was Robert, covered with a beautiful AIDS quilt, a rose resting on his breast. I bent over him, pressed my head against his, and whispered, "O Robert, my man, my man, O Robert." And then I knelt at the side of his bed and wept and wept. The paradox is that, in the end, the little guy had been stripped of everything but was surrounded by the dearest of possessions, his friends.

September 1, Friday

Mary Sue, Joe, Mara, Michael, Sr. Kate, and I went to the coast this morning and, after a brief liturgy of prayer and readings, scattered Robert's cremated remains into the Pacific Ocean, as he had requested. The ceremony took place on a stretch of beach where the Nestucca River flows into the Pacific. After we finished, we stood, six across, our arms around one another, silently gazing into the crashing surf, commending Robert's spirit to God. I moved through those emotions connected to him, alternately aware of what a strange and wonderful person-gift he was to me and of that gentle and painful resignation that prevails when someone I have known and loved has died. In such moments, all I can do is fall back on the most fundamental law of my life: God is, God gives, God calls us back to God's heart.

When I returned from the beach, I opened the box that Robert had left me. It contained a few personal papers, a couple of books, and some pottery items that he had loved. On top of everything was this note:

My dearest Father Gary,

I cannot adequately put into words what your friendship has meant to me over the past few years. You have been my steady rock in the raging storm. You've been the father to me that I always wished for when I was growing up. You've given so much, and I know you've got so much more to give. Your ministry has just begun. When the time comes to depart this earth, rest assured that you made the difference in many troubled souls' lives. God bless you, Father Gary.

If all goes well, I'll be watching over you.

All my love,

Robert

He has.

chapter twelve

ASHES IN THE WIND:

DEATH IN THE WORLD OF THE

HOMELESS

I always feel so inadequate when I am in the
presence of someone who is dying. I know that
I am just an instrument to prepare the way,
a witness to the presence of the holy.

He does not break the crushed reed,
nor quench the wavering flame.

ISAIAH 42:3

In the course of a day at Outreach
Ministry, at the Macdonald Center, at the Sisters of the Road Café,
and at Rose Haven (a women-only drop-in center), staff members
see many people who come in bearing any number of physical and
emotional afflictions. These afflictions include:

diabetes-induced infections in feet and legs
black eyes caused by physical abuse
the flu
fury over not being able to access the system
devastation over being HIV positive
long-term alcoholism and its debilitating side effects
the need to be held
the need to talk
smoldering anger over a condescending and infuriating landlord
murmuring, maddening voices in one's head, brought on by
    schizophrenia
frustration with a body that will not function correctly
discouragement born of self-disgust
chills due to lack of clothing in cold weather
dysfunctional speech patterns caused by a violent head injury
malnutrition and its side effects
grief over yet another hotel death—maybe just down the hall
heroin withdrawal
the slow crush of loneliness
the torture of chemotherapy
the indifference of a family
delusions and accompanying fears
the weariness of old age
pain caused by a manipulative and rejecting lover
helplessness caused by not having an income
the fear of having to sleep on the streets
the need to weep

Underneath all this painful stuff is the clinging reality of being poor, which is, in most cases, a sentence for life.

It is important that all these afflictions be dealt with not casually or with distraction but with awareness and, one hopes, with the maximum amount of attention and respect. The residents of Old Town, many of whom have been discarded by family and society, need to know that in spite of all their jagged edges and psychological and physical brokenness, caring staff members will meet them where they are with attention and concern. We can do this because we suffer from our own kind of poverty and are not above the breaks and bruises of life. If we kid ourselves in this regard, we are fools; if we accept it and enter into the lives of other suffering human beings, we touch the holy—in the other and in ourselves.

Everyone knows that in those difficult moments in life, it is important—so important—that other people recognize our weaknesses and take care not to quench the flame of hope that barely flickers within us. It is important that people meet us, love us, embrace us, bind us up, and encourage us—in all of our confusion—to step into the next part of our journey. Such presence can nourish us and give our hope a chance to break out into the open and live. Then, even if all the staring cynics and self-absorbed scoffers write us off as losers, we can rest in the truth that an authentic person took the time to care. In the presence of this kind of love, we are able to say—as we hope the people who come to OMB or Rose Haven or the Macdonald Center or Sisters of the Road Café can say—"They believe me, they love me, they discover strength in my wounds." In this, Isaiah's vision is fulfilled.

I experience this most poignantly when I see the care that some staff members pour onto men and women who are dying in their SROs. The ill persons want to remain there as long as they can because they know that their real family consists of the people who check in on them, bathe them, and attend to their most private needs. It is no easy thing to see a person die, slowly. But to see obscure people dying in obscure hotel rooms, yet cared for as if they were the most important people in the world—what an amazing sight. They are treated as if they were someone's father or mother. But that is exactly the point: they are. Having no family, they have a family. The operative mantra of care is No kin, my kin.

When I see people caring for those who are dying in the SROs, it reminds me of a stunning truth of the often dreary world of the streets: No person, whoever he or she is or wherever he or she lives, is denied the grasp of God's heart. We are cherished by God, hunted by God, redeemed by God. And having experienced this, we are reminded that we are called to be bearers of God's love and truth, and, as bearers, we are to bring that love and truth into our culture, where there exist the bruises and flickering flames caused by poverty, lack of education, poor health care, homelessness, loneliness, racism, and injustice. All of our brothers and sisters are *not* treated equally, and the least deserve more.

· · ·

They discovered Bobby's body in the Danmore Hotel on the Tuesday after Father's Day. I arrived shortly after the medical examiner began his preliminary examination. A client of Outreach Ministry for two years, Bobby had failed to come in on Monday. Missing a day was not unusual for him, but he was a fragile guy, so we made sure the hotel checked his room. He had died over the weekend, one of the many poor who live and die in the SROs located in the downtown Portland area. Four died in the Foster Hotel last month; a Nam vet died in the Estate Hotel last Sunday; an elderly woman killed herself recently at a nearby apartment complex. All were alone when they died.

When I came into Bobby's apartment, the medical examiner informed me that he had been dead for almost forty-eight hours. He was two days into rigor mortis. I knelt on the floor of the dark and smelly room, next to his half-naked body. On his upper torso, pools of blood had gathered underneath his skin, resembling gigantic birthmarks. There was a burned-down joint locked between two of his fingers. On the bed were letters from his cherished grandmother in Illinois, and a jacket was hung neatly over the back of the room's solitary chair. The vodka bottles scattered about the room indicated that Bobby had blasted himself into a furious, final, and fatal relapse. He was thirty-three. Cause of death: chronic alcoholism.

I looked into his lifeless eyes and whispered his name, commending him to God.

Anyone who knew Bobby could never shrug him off as just a drunk, another boozer who had died alone in a run-down, sleazy SRO. Certainly our Outreach Ministry staff couldn't. Nor could the many people who gathered in our little storefront office for his memorial service a week after his death. There, at the service, friends gave raw and eloquent testimony to his humanity. Moving beyond his inconsistencies, his mental illness, and his substance abuse, they craf-ted words that revealed the deeper truth and story of the man's heart.

Professionals from the Hooper Detox Center affectionately remembered him and, in the same breath, recalled the tortured nights of detoxification they had spent with him, watching him wrestle with his angels and demons. One of Bobby's acquaintances from the Danmore recalled Bobby's care for people who were "lost." A woman friend spoke of his "gentleness." A wise companion recalled that "Bobby was a light for others but could not be a light for himself." One member from his Alcoholics Anonymous group wept over the loss of a young man who was "like my own son." A staff person offered her favorite poem, befitting a memorial; another, off in a corner, wept quietly. The majority of those at the service chose not to say anything; they were silent witnesses to their love for him and his capacity to make friends.

Many of us smiled as we reflected on Bobby's sense of humor and on how it tickled him to seduce us into laughter with a straight face. I was particularly vulnerable to his ways. Shortly after meeting him for the first time and looking over his military discharge papers, I asked him what he did with the Special Forces. He said he couldn't tell me because of the top secret nature of the missions in which he had been involved. He often used that kind of language when I would ask him questions about the most mundane things, such as how was he doing, or what did he have for breakfast, or how was his date the previous night. "Can't tell you, Father, it's top secret. Jesuits would understand that. Besides, if I told you, well, quite frankly, I'd have to kill you." It cracked me up every time, and he would feed off my laughter. His nutty routine never failed to hook me. Indeed, his gleaming-eyed sense of humor could help me make sense of an otherwise crummy day.

Of course, there were moments when the man was a frustrating and consummate jerk. The drinking led to unacceptable behavior and lots of garbage talk, and on some occasions he made very dumb decisions. Finding housing for Bobby, or any other ill and volatile person, could almost be a mission impossible. When he first became a client at Outreach, his impatience with us was loud and aggressive, like a buzz saw. He was a very obnoxious man. But he grew. So did we. Eventually, we rejoiced with him over his progress toward sobriety and wholeness, and we grieved when he staggered and relapsed.

We decided that it was important to gather as a church and offer prayers for Bobby and his family, who lived on the East Coast. We did so with a street liturgy that reflected our respect and love for him. And though society might have dismissed him as just another insufferable street alcoholic and a corpse dispatched to the morgue—as so many of his SRO brothers and sisters are dismissed and dispatched—it was crucial that we proclaim to the world an opposite and far more passionate message: that he was a child of God, a creature of the Creator, unique, special, beloved.

Ah, we shall miss you, Bobby Brown. We shall miss you.

■ ■ ■

What happens when SRO residents die and they have absolutely no family to attend to their cremated remains? The task is left to their only family, the little band of staff members who have looked after them over the years. Today the OMB staff went to the Oregon coast to scatter the ashes of Harry, Lloyd, Karen, and Gary.

Like a little caravan of desert pilgrims, bundled up to protect ourselves from the elements, the eight of us moved south on the windswept beach, bearing the four boxes of ashes. We stopped a hundred yards in, solitary figures on the late-winter shore, and gathered silently in a circle, holding hands. I led us in prayers for the three brothers and the sister whose ashes we were commending to Mother Earth and whose souls we were commending to the Creator. We remembered a special quality about each of the deceased. The tears of care and love that were shed struck me as more enormous than the panorama of ocean and shoreline that surrounded us. Through Scripture, I reminded us all of the ultimate dignity that each one of these precious human beings had by virtue of being creatures and children of God:

> *For Zion was saying, "Yahweh has abandoned me,*
> *the Lord has forgotten me."*
> *Does a woman forget her baby at the breast,*
> *or fail to cherish the son of her womb?*
> *Yet even if these forget,*
> *I will never forget you.*

See, I have branded you on the palms of my hands.
ISAIAH 49:14–16

Our prayers concluded, we broke up into four teams of two and scattered the ashes at the point where the ocean's waves kissed the beach. Tiny earth-hugging trails of sand were blowing out toward the water, moving swiftly across the beach like sidewinder snakes. Jesse, the veteran caretaker for so many of the members, captured the moment, describing these trails of sand as "spirits of nature following after the great spirits whose ashes we have cast into the sea."

■ ■ ■

Can you not buy two sparrows for a penny? And yet
not one falls to the ground without your Father
knowing. Why, every hair on your head has been
counted. So there is no need to be afraid; you are
worth more than hundreds of sparrows.
MATTHEW 10:29–31

We hadn't seen Enrique in a few days. He was not in his room, not on the streets. We checked the jail and the hospitals. Not there. We finally tracked him down through the medical examiner's office: he was in the morgue. While crossing Front Street on a dark and rainy December night, he was struck by a car. He was killed instantly—probably never knew what hit him. Officials had to identify him through fingerprints because he was not carrying ID. There were no relatives to inform, no addresses to check out, no best friends to be contacted. Nobody. In the end, having located him, we were his family. We mourned him, we memorialized him, and we will attend to his sacred remains, as a family should do.

He was Hispanic, spoke very little English, was in his sixties, and was probably originally from Mexico. Nobody knew his date or place of birth for sure, and quite frankly, such personal questions were lost on him—a result of the wear and tear he had endured over the years. Enrique was short of stature and thin as a rail and had a face dominated by hollow cheeks, sunken eyes, and a scraggly beard. He was habitually dressed in a mountain of shirts and jackets. He always wore a happy smile and was agreeable to every overture made to him, whether he understood it or not. For a long time—who knows how long—his home was the streets. In fact, he came to Outreach just a few years ago, after he was moved out of his residence of several years, a spot underneath a bridge over Front Street.

He couldn't shake the habits he had formed living alone on the streets for as long as he had. Recently, I had to ask him to leave OMB premises because cockroaches were crawling out from underneath his coat collar. When we inspected the coat outside, we discovered that he was a walking cockroach den. And these weren't babies. They were big, fat, and well fed. Enrique, in his usual state of cheerful incomprehension, smiled, nodded, and shuffled off toward his hotel room, where he apparently fed them. Feed the roaches and they won't bother you in the night. Years under the bridges will teach you that.

We could never obtain subsistence money for Enrique from the Social Security Administration because there was no record of his birth. Eventually we hooked him up with the state's General Assistance program. He received a very modest amount of monthly money, which covered his rent, with only a little change left over. But Enrique had lived on nothing for most of his life.

The Outreach staff and a few others cared for him; this was evident at our staff memorial service for him. He had what most of us spend a lifetime trying to achieve: openness to everyone around him, freedom from judgment, and no walls for people to battle through. His eyes and voice were always welcoming, and his presence never dominated or threatened. In his unobtrusive way, he contributed to the landscape of peace that we try to create for our members, who often have harsh and difficult lives.

Sometimes we encounter individuals who help us locate the intersection of the divine and the human. They break open our hearts, and we understand God's care for all because they are simple and lovable, worthy and good—a gift to us all. Nothing they do distracts us. Everything they do enhances us. They lead us to the intrinsic beauty in every human being. Enrique was such an individual.

■ ■ ■

Before he became debilitated by cancer, OMB client Richard and I did a few things together. He was a skinny old man with scars on his chin and eyebrows, the result of a lifetime of drunken falls and brawls. He did not suffer fools and was notorious for his cantankerous attitude. Inside, though, he was a marshmallow, like Oscar the Grouch on *Sesame Street*, and if I pushed the right button he would warm up. That tactic was also used by others who had come to love him over his many years in Old Town.

He was a baseball fan, so when I suggested that we attend a professional baseball game, he was pumped up for weeks. He had told me during the course of our friendship that he had been quite the jock in high school and college—his glory days before he began to drink heavily and before life became an inexorable path of cheap wine, jail, detox clinics, dumpy hotel rooms, sidewalk sleeping, and empty relationships.

As we sat in the bleachers enjoying the game, Richard—as sober as he had been in weeks—kept dropping little bits of insider information, demonstrating that he had been around the bases a few times himself. Throughout the game, whenever a Portland player would come up to bat, he'd size the batter up and inevitably conclude with the same subtle analysis: "Father, he is going to knock the fucking ball out of the fucking ballpark!" For *every* Portland player he said this, in *every* inning. I nodded in noncommittal affirmation.

Of course, it never happened, and Portland was being shut out. But then, in the eighth inning, Portland, scoreless, was batting, and the bases were loaded. Richard turned to me, squinting his eyes shrewdly, and made his usual prediction—this, with the worst Portland hitter at bat. And then—*ka-blaaaam!* the most pathetic hitter blasts the fucking ball out of the fucking ballpark. Gone!

Richard high-fived me again and again and solicited the admiration of the surrounding fans by informing them that he had actually called the home run. I never heard the end of it. On the bus ride home, he kept shaking his head in disbelief and self-admiration, turning to me periodically and saying, "Didn't I tell you, Father, didn't I tell you?" And, of course, for days afterward he informed all comers at his hotel of his remarkable display of prescience, capping it all off with the indisputable clincher: "Ask Father Gary, *he* was there, *he'll* tell you." Yep, I had witnessed the miraculous prophecy.

On another occasion we went to a big local air show. Richard had done a tour in the air force, loved planes, and was very knowledgeable about them. My big fear was that he would stash a couple of pints somewhere on his skinny body and then pound them in a Porta Potty and we would be booted from the festivities. He agreed not to do so, and I said I would buy us an occasional beer.

What I remember most vividly about that day is how the U.S. Navy flight demonstration squadron, the Blue Angels, surprised me when they zoomed onto the scene from behind us. Richard's first reaction was to laugh at me, because their sudden and explosive arrival had utterly startled me. He had warned me earlier of the possible thunderous arrival of the Angels, so he thought my reaction was hilarious. The old veteran laughing at the rookie. Then suddenly his face changed from amusement and joy to sadness and tears. I asked him about it, and he said that those jets always made him realize what he might have been had he "not become a wino."

One afternoon, after the cancer had worsened to the point of keeping him bedridden, I went to his room and found him lying half in and half out of his bed, his hands locked on an empty paper cup. He had spilled the entire cup of water and had reached down to get more. But because he was in such a weakened state, he had become stuck in that position. He hadn't eaten substantially in three weeks, and as a result he looked ancient. I lifted him up gently, swung him back around into his bed, and made sure that he was in a more or less comfortable position. He looked at me blankly and weakly said thanks. I asked him how he felt. He smiled and said, "Somewhere between a musty old biscuit and a slice of moldy green bread."

The night before he died, I went over to his room to pray the Prayers for the Dying with him. At this point he was nearly comatose, and nurses were coming in periodically to check on him, as were Outreach staffers Jesse and Laurie. No OMB member who is dying in his or her room is loved more than those two can love.

When I walked into Richard's room that night, I was surprised to find it full of Native Americans and some hotel residents. It was a miniconvention of Richard's fans. His last wife was a full-blooded Sioux, and he had—in a long stretch of sobriety—helped raise her three daughters. She died many years ago, and he never recovered from the grief of losing her. All the daughters were present, as were some of their friends who had known Richard. It turns out that they "knew" this was it; they were there to spend the night. One asked if we could pray, so I led a litany to which they all responded. It was a pure and wonderful moment: everyone was seated around Richard's bed, and the only sounds of the universe were the voices of devotion and Richard's labored breathing.

These are times of raw humility for me. I always feel so inadequate when I am in the presence of someone who is dying. What can I say that doesn't sound wooden and artificial; what is the "priestly" thing to say? Inevitably, the faith of the surrounding people carries and sustains me, and I know that I am just an instrument to prepare the way, a witness to the presence of the holy, however unholy I feel.

Richard died the next morning at six o'clock, mercifully and in his sleep, surrounded by his faithful friends.

■ ■ ■

Martha, eighty-one years young, died in her room recently. She was an extraordinary woman. High quality. I often saw her walking around on the streets, all hunched over, shuffling along. She was always good for a greeting and a self-deprecating crack about her uncooperative body. She was forever solicitous for my well-being ("Now you be careful down here, Father").

I led the memorial service for her in the lobby of her hotel. Nancy, a resident who takes it upon herself to research the lives of the deceased, discovered that Martha was a published poet and read one of her poems. Other residents offered affectionate recollections about her, which are the greatest compliments this side of the heart of God.

Charlie, a quiet man who rarely speaks, rose from his chair and launched his words like an arrow: straight, clean, true. "She was one of the finest ladies I ever knew."

Sitting in the room and soaking it all up were her nephew, David, and his daughter. He clearly was touched by the dignity that surrounded him. In one short burst, he learned more about his aunt and the love people had for her than he had in all the years he had been distant from her.

. . .

I visited Gary and had a one-way conversation with him as he lay in his hospital bed in a coma. I had no idea if he could hear me, but I talked to him anyway, rubbing his hand and arm gently. He had been in a coma for seven days, kept alive by machines and a jungle of tubes. A week earlier, in an obscure southeast Portland alley, he'd been struck on the head by a "blunt instrument."

As I sat next to him and stroked his arm, I remembered—for the two of us—his life with Outreach Ministry, sometimes shaking my head in disapproval, other times smiling with affection. He had been an OMB member for three and a half years. His disabilities—all a result of his alcoholism—had been a part of his life for many years. His drinking problem was so serious that his rap sheet was as long as I am tall; most of his arrests had to do with public intoxication. We had lots to talk about.

He died the day after my visit, having never regained consciousness. Murdered at the age of forty-nine.

Gary had many talents. He held an Associate in arts. He was a journeyman welder. He was eccentric, audacious, uninhibited, and outspoken—and contagious in his joy. He could be a royal pain, too, directing his harmless nastiness at a variety of people. Once, he had an altercation with the night clerk at his SRO, in which the guy bit Gary on the thumb. Gary's reflection: "Father, I'd rather be bitten by a dog than by that asshole."

Gary was a world-class dumpster diver, driven by an entrepreneurial spirit that was tailored to the garbage world. He was not just a snooper looking for cans to sell, but a man with a mission: books to sell; copper and aluminum to recycle; radios, TVs, and computers to repair; personal items to give as gifts. He was the king of his country, systematically conquering it: collecting, trading or selling the booty, and saving the unique. If he found a dead cat, he would bury it; if he found a live cat, he would take it to the animal shelter. He kept some items the way most people keep trophies, as objects to be admired. He was not self-absorbed in his quest. All OMB staff and all of Gary's friends were beneficiaries of his sensitive gift-giving. He once presented Maria with an album of Gregorian chant, given on the occasion of her mother's death. He said it was the kind of thing "that I would want to listen to, if I felt sad." He often brought beat-up books to me because he knew I liked to read.

Once, when he was in the hospital about to have a leg operation, he called me with some important instructions. "Would you mind, Father, locating a bag of mine? I left it at detox, and it contains a set of false teeth, loaded with gold, silver, and platinum. I found them in a dumpster. Uppers and lowers. Can you believe that, Father, uppers *and* lowers. I need them." It seems that he was going to cannibalize the gold and silver from the false teeth and transfer the metals to his own teeth. He thought he'd look pretty good, and it would go along with the patched-up leg—all part of what he was calling his "human transformation."

He had a sense of humor that was infectious. Upon invitation he would make up a song—melody and verses—on the spot and perform his music as easily as if he were reciting multiplication tables. I prompted him once, "Sing me a song about crankcase oil, Gary."

"No problem, Father." And he proceeded to bellow out some song that had crankcase oil as its major theme. I can't help but say that the whole song—both the melody and the message—had a crankcase-oil quality to it.

Once, he walked into the OMB office with a couple of bottles of cologne, products of his latest dive, and proceeded to anoint some of us with it. For days he reeked of perfume and dumpsters, a rare combination.

Gary was fiercely loyal and frequently looked out for others, whether they were street friends, staff people, or landlords who put up with his junk-collecting habits. At our Outreach Ministry memorial service for Gary, we all had a chance to reflect on him. It was there that we experienced the depth and power of his impact on our hearts. Gary, for all his bad and good moments, really got to us. In his remarkable way, he managed to share all his many gifts with us. As we commended him to God, we prayed and wept, because he had touched us. He knew us all by name, so we could testify to God how Gary had chosen to linger with each one of us in some unique and enduring manner while we knew him. In those moments we received some of the finest gifts a human being could give.

■ ■ ■

Once in a while Jim would track me down to talk. He was a self-educated man who lived in one of the local SROs and supported himself by washing windows for local businesses. He was active in trying to improve the quality of life for Old Town residents. He and I sometimes had a beer at the Starting Point Tavern, a local hangout for a lot of the poor in the area and a business that had survived the gentrification that was slowly leaking into Old Town.

Jim came up to me one day and informed me that the "Little One," Becky, a regular bartender at the tavern, had shot herself. Right there, at the bar. She was forty. "Would you do some kind of memorial service for her?" he asked me.

"Of course. Where?"

"At the bar."

A few days later, at 10:30 in the morning, I did my first and only memorial service in a tavern. It was a small place, with the bar itself running the length of one side of the room and about a dozen booths shoehorned into the other side. I took my place in front of the jukebox, at the far end of the room, using the bar as a prop for my Bible. I greeted everyone and nervously began a service of prayers, readings, and reflections. All the booths were full of people, as were the stools at the bar, and already some pitchers of beer had been poured.

Knowing something of Becky's solicitude for all the tavern's clients, I began with the tenth chapter of John, the parable of the good shepherd. I tried to connect her care for the brothers and sisters of Old Town, with all their warts and wonders, to the care God had for her in all the known and unknown troubles in her life. Preaching on the occasion of a suicide is not easy, but I tried to preempt any of Becky's decisions about her life with the decisions that God has made for all of us. If we are lost, I stressed, God will hunt us down—in love—like the good shepherd, to the last moment.

At one point, as I always do when I lead Old Town memorials, I invited everyone present to reflect on the deceased and, if they had anything to say, to please share. I did this with a little trepidation, knowing that there were a few intoxicated people present among the majority of sober and sad faces—which is to say, I knew I was inviting rambling and disconnected statements. But what emerged was great appreciation of the Little One and of her ability to listen to them when they were in trouble.

From the back corner: "How many hearts—broken by life and love—were shared with her? Count me as one of them."

Next to me, a weeping woman said, "I couldn't tell you how many countless crummy hours, in this crummy old tavern, Becky heard my crummy story."

Another said: "Why do such good people feel so bad about themselves? I will miss her goodness."

Then there were customers who started talking about Becky but wound up rambling about themselves. One guy, incredibly, began lamenting the fact that his team wasn't participating in the Super Bowl. But the more focused Starting Point customers gently shushed these self-absorbed individuals, and the floor was given back to me.

The tears on the faces in the tavern that day were a silent testimony to the love that many felt for this woman, whose presence and touch had carried them through painful moments.

In the end, we all joined hands and prayed the Our Father. I concluded with a prayer commending the Little One to the Good Shepherd.

After the service, a couple of people approached me and wanted to talk. They wore looks on their faces that I have seen before, often in public places where some kind of religious event has taken place. They were trying to adjust to the shock of a Catholic priest in a tavern using God talk and bringing greater meaning to an event. They were aware that Becky's death could have been handled with a shrug of the shoulders and a toast: "Here's to our Becky, who blew her brains out." But another kind of life had penetrated them during that memorial service, like a solitary ray of sun in the darkness.

They were moved by the event and by the shock of me, but something else had happened, too: a mystery had touched them, and subconsciously they knew that there was a relationship between the event and the mystery. This unarticulated awareness disclosed itself in their questions: Are you really a priest? Do you do this much, Father? Does the church really do this? Is God for real? Can God love someone like me, who never goes to church?

And I, for my part, knew that God was on the move, that the mystery of grace is mediated through concrete situations. The more concrete the situation—like a memorial in a "crummy old tavern"—the more powerful it is. There are no rules for when or how God begins a relationship. I know only that it happens.

■ ■ ■

I was asked by one of our OMB staff persons, who is gay, if I would consider officiating at the annual Memorial Day service that the gay community holds down at Riverfront Park in a designated area overlooking the Willamette River. I agreed to do the service, thinking how ironic it was that I should be doing it—given my latent homophobia. As a priest, of course, I knew I should be there with these men and women. As a child of our homophobic culture, I had mixed emotions.

For most of my life I had my own versions of the stereotypical prejudices toward homosexuality, a result of the usual macho-guy baggage. I told dirty jokes, made snorting observations of gay couples ("Look at those fags"), and was indifferent to the theological and existential questions of gay men and women. *Questions* may be the wrong word; how about *agony*? In my guy-talk world, Jesuit and otherwise, I had a repulsion for any kind of romantic relationship that was not clearly defined as heterosexual.

I am not sure at what point my attitude began to change; it could have been the result of any number of things: the close friendships I had formed with a couple of gay men and women, the long talks with gay Jesuits, the acquaintance of street people who struggled to understand themselves as homosexual. Whatever the catalyst, I came to find it less and less possible to relate to my gay friends on the basis of past viewpoints. I was unwilling to be seduced by homophobic attitudes. So, as I joined the crowd at Riverfront Park on Memorial Day, I was conscious of both my history and my care and appreciation for the brothers and sisters who had asked me to be there.

The Memorial Day service began, as usual, with everyone assembling at a local gay pub, bearing bouquets of flowers. From there we proceeded two blocks to the river, where, in a large semicircle and with me leading the prayers, we remembered the dead. On either side of me stood the bearers of love, bound up in the precious memories of friends who had died. In the case of this community, many of the deceased had died young. The specter of AIDS hung over the gathered as surely as the river flowed quietly in front of us. For many present, a whole generation of their friends had been decimated by this disease. It was like living on an eroding beach. And yet their hope was bending over backward trying to make sense of it all. How do you cope with life when best friends are gone? Whom do you count on?

I read from Isaiah and offered a few words on the reality of the one whom we must all count on, in life and death.

> *I have called you by your name, you are mine.*
> *Should you pass through the sea, I will be with you;*
> *or through rivers, they will not swallow you up.*
> *Should you walk through fire, you will not be*
>   *scorched*
> *and the flames will not burn you. . . .*
> *Because you are precious in my eyes,*
> *because you are honored and I love you.*
>   ISAIAH 43:1–2, 4

As I looked around, trying to craft some words appropriate to the occasion and thinking of Isaiah's words about another little community that lived on the edges, I couldn't help but think that the half-circle was a functional metaphor. The gay and lesbian community exists and moves on the edges of the circle of our culture. I know we say that we have a diverse culture and that all are welcome—even the church is now saying this, nervously—but theirs is a community that continues to live on the outskirts. I guess I was feeling some of the pain of it all in that moment, in spite of the strength and endurance I was receiving from the surrounding group of men and women.

In the solitude of the morning we concluded our service, joining hands in a final silent prayer. Then, individually, as couples, or as small groups, we proceeded to a platform overlooking the Willamette. Silently, we dropped our flowers into the river as it moved north toward the Columbia, which was making its powerful way to the Pacific.

Back at the bar, a small buffet had been prepared. People kept coming up to me, wanting to talk. It was one of those mysterious moments in which my priesthood allows me to bridge factors that would normally keep people apart. I thought of that line in 2 Corinthians in which Paul says, "He has entrusted to us the news that they are reconciled. So we are ambassadors for Christ; it is as though God were appealing through us, and the appeal that we make in Christ's name is: be reconciled to God" (2 Corinthians 5:19–20).

And one point I heard the words "Can I talk to you for a moment, Father?" and there he was, holding a plate of mixed fruit and a glass of Chardonnay, a young gay man wanting to share something with me, not because I was a good guy but because I was a Jesuit priest. As we talked, the heart of this stranger came barging into the open and was simultaneously unburdened and reclaimed. I see this happen in jails, in hotel rooms, after Masses in churches from Portland to Bolivia, during and after fund-raiser cocktail parties, and in every nook and cranny on the streets. It is unnerving. Yet, it is to be expected. I realize that I am involved in a vocation that is so much bigger than I can understand. The spirit of God will use me as an agent of reconciliation, no matter how resistant or unprepared or prejudiced I may be.

■ ■ ■

Harry died suddenly today. A heart attack felled him shortly after a fire burned down part of his house. He had called me between the fire and the attack. When I called back, of course, there was no answer. He was dead.

Harry was one of the most loyal volunteers in the Macdonald Center program that sent people to visit with residents in the old hotels. At the Thursday afternoon reflection groups for Macdonald Center staff and volunteers, he always had something rich to say, born of his own kind of suffering. He was a nervous man with a nervous machine-gun laugh who specialized in seeing as many people as possible in his afternoon visits. He traveled with a wonderful wheelchair-bound woman, Rosie, whose cerebral palsy has severely handicapped her movement and speech. This was no problem for Harry, who became the world's greatest Rosie translator and a most loving friend. One of the most delightful sights in Old Town was of the two of them steamrolling down the sidewalks—Harry pushing at top speed, yakking endlessly, and Rosie, hair flying and laughing hysterically—on their way to visit with all the old-timers.

Harry is dead, gone like last moment's breath. There did not seem to be a bad bone in him, in all of his excitable, Buddhist-inspired caring ways. Mary Sue, the Macdonald Center director, the deep feeler, was broken up by the news, as were her staff and volunteers.

Show me how I can be present to all this grief, O God. And Harry, pray for us, that we might imitate your selfless, unaffected care.

■ ■ ■

Rosie returned to the Macdonald Center today, a few weeks after we lost Harry. She was wheeled into the basement about ten minutes after we had begun our Thursday group. It was a

poignant and breathtaking occasion, so soon after the death of
Harry, her best buddy. She wept and then talked about her grief.
In spite of her speech impediment, Rosie transfixed us with her
soaring expressions of love and grief. The group was impaled on
her heart.

Is anything more devastating than the loss of a best friend?
The mourning runs so deep that words miss the mark. They are
nothing but a shadow of the truth. How can anyone else understand the unique contribution someone's best friend made to his
or her life? When a best friend dies, a piece of us dies, too, and
we become like a separated Siamese twin, once joined at the
heart to a soul mate and now cut apart and living in another
galaxy. But the blood of the soul mate still flows in our veins, and
our hearts still bear the indelible imprint of another heart. I
think they always will.

At one point Rosie said to me, "I better shut up; I'm taking your
job."

I replied, "No group has ever been led so gracefully, Rosie."

Her honesty, delivered to a group such as ours, was the stuff of a
sacred moment; it was raw, fragile, and, like Rosie, irrepressible. In
a strange way, listening to her was like hearing a great piece of
music or an extraordinary musician for the first time: we simply
had never heard anything like this before. She took us to a higher
level of human communication, pushing our hearts to that frontier
of wonder, which to that point we had never crossed.

I thought later that Rosie's sharing had led me to an epiphany
about what the church should be. There we were, sitting in that
little circle around our suffering sister and hurling ourselves into
the breach of her pain, absorbing some of it but not robbing her of
the task of dealing with what she must deal with. And she—so
poor—was teaching us about love and dignity. It was a tragic and
amazing moment. Harry, her Harry, our Harry, was gone.

■ ■ ■

I officiated at memorial services for two men at two different hotels, men I didn't know. I had to learn of them through the words and faces of those who knew them. Paul, fifty-three, was dead for three days before they found him. He was a friend to several individuals for many years, someone who frequently grocery shopped for SRO residents who were not mobile. He was generous and made time for everyone.

"He would give me his newspaper, sometimes before he had completed it," said Clarence, a fellow resident, a ninety-year-old retired Methodist minister.

I used the passage from Luke about the widow of Nain, connecting Paul's care for others with how Jesus went to people in need, especially the widow. How often Paul did this at the Foster Hotel, being attentive and helpful. He was especially kind to one disabled person, caring for him for four years until the man shot himself.

The second funeral was for Randy, a combat veteran of the Vietnam War who came back, like so many of his companions, with a steady stream of terrifying memories and an addiction to dope. His wife died of pneumonia shortly after his return, and his only son was lost to neglect and, subsequently, Child Protective Services.

Present at this service was a handful of people, the most touching being a tearful Kathy, his former girlfriend. She looked as though she'd suffered her share of pain, even now, seeking a shelter for herself and her little boy, Jesse. Randy had been good to her, and in spite of all her pain, there was a warmth and openness about her face when she spoke of him. The people who spoke after my remarks gave rich, eloquent testimony to a man whom I will never meet in this life. He was forty-five. Dead of a heart attack. Dead in his room for a week before he was found.

■ ■ ■

It is always a challenging and humbling experience to do a service in a hotel lobby for someone I never knew, with mourning people whom I usually do not know. People hand over to me a tremendous amount of power in these moments, believing that I can bring some order and meaning into the chaos and darkness of death.

I don't kid myself; I know I can't do this by myself. So I do my own kind of handing over. I hand over the mystery of death to God, and I hand myself over to the mystery of my vocation: to be there for these folks, living and dead. I am the divining rod in their search for the holy in their lives. I have confidence in these moments, because I know that my task is a simple one. I am to extract—from all the sadness of a lonely death, from the bleakness of a cheap hotel lobby, and from the words and tears of all present—this sacred truth: that the deceased are the sacred children of God and that, in the end, God's love trumps everything.

■ ■ ■

Then some men appeared, carrying on a bed a
paralyzed man whom they were trying to bring in
and lay down in front of him. But as the crowd made
it impossible to find a way of getting him in, they
went up on to the flat roof and lowered him and his
stretcher down through the tiles into the middle of the
gathering, in front of Jesus.

LUKE 5:18–19

Before multiple sclerosis confined him to his bed, Wells used to drop in on me, traveling from Spokane in his specially adapted van, with steering wheel controls and a lift that placed him and his wheelchair on the sidewalk. It was his way of being supportive of the work I do and of nurturing our friendship, which went back more than forty years. On these visits he referred to me as a "Roofer," a metaphor he used for those who care for the needy, based on the Scripture passage from Luke 5. In addition to his constant moral support, he sent money for "soup, soap, and socks" to be used for the poor of the streets.

I received word of Wells's end on a Friday night from a Los Angeles Roofer. Wells had died an hour before in his Spokane residence. The slow torture of multiple sclerosis had finally killed him.

That damn insidious disease began who knows when. Symptoms appeared a dozen years ago, long after our college days at Santa Clara, his brief stint with the Jesuits, his doctoral studies, and the birth of his two daughters. Once the long haul with MS commenced, he went from a few awkward inconveniences to falling on his face; from a cane to a wheelchair. Eventually he found himself flat on his back. He used to say, "It's like being buried alive, Gar, one spoonful of dirt at a time."

We chatted on the phone periodically, especially when he couldn't make his trips to Portland anymore. I visited him whenever I was in Spokane. He lived alone next to the Spokane River but was visited daily by a variety of care providers—Roofers all. Our visits were quality time. There were a few yuks; some tears over the darkness, frustration, and loneliness of life; and the tender and mutual trust of two friends working through the raw stuff of life, faith, relationships, and the madness of MS. He always made time for me, his gaunt and bony face attentive, solicitous, thoughtful.

Wells had a personal meaning for the expression "the Roofers," and he used it to refer to a group of men who were, for the most part, former Jesuits—1960s vintage—and who collectively decided to ensure that Wells's final years and last blast of life would be taken care of financially. His pension and insurance could not cover all the expenses of his home and the kind of care he needed. So each month they would mail in money to a designated person who, in turn, would write the necessary checks.

It was a mixed group, these Roofers: lawyers, physicians, blue collars, teachers, psychologists, architects, priests. They were—by their act of roofing—extraordinary people, yet very ordinary, comfortable with the obscurity of their mission of love, just like their Gospel counterparts who worked behind the scenes to attend to a wounded brother.

I celebrated the funeral Mass with another Jesuit friend, Pat, as Wells had requested. Indeed, he had the whole liturgy planned out, including, of course, the Gospel story of the paralytic man and his devoted friends. The lead Roofer, Tony, gently spoke of the story in his homily:

This passage meant a lot to Wells. He mailed it to his friends. He picked it for today. For him it was a picture of the last years of his life. He called all of us here his Roofers. Those of us who phoned him, wrote to him, visited him, saved him a place on the gym floor, prayed for him, spent the night with him, thought about him, cared about him—all Roofers.

We were involved in his life. We look at ourselves—friends, family, caretakers—and we see that we were indeed the people from the Gospel: packing him on his litter, down the alleys, across the river, up the stairs, to the very roof. We pulled off the tiles. We hardly had a choice. He was yanking on us to do so.

He really knew what it meant to be a Roofer. Most of us didn't have a clue. We Roofers just did as we were told. We carried him around and then up to the roof.

We were never embarrassed by it. It really wasn't too hard. He was pretty light, after all. A banana and a burrito a day for four years. He didn't complain. His spirits were pretty good most of the time. Just bring me here. Do this. Do that. Bring me right up to the roof. You can do it. Now tear off those tiles, and look down there and see if Jesus is there. Okay, now lower me down. Carefully.

No questions asked. Okay, Wells. Here we go, buddy. No problem. Easy does it. Down you go.

And then the universe stops still. The Lord looks up toward the roof and sees us, the Roofers. And we are amazed. That's what it's all about.

Wells used to say, "My vocation, during this part of my life, is to lead people to God by having them take care of me."

It worked. Our hearts opened. He showed us faith; he showed us caring; he showed us forgiveness; he showed us kindness. He led the way to God.

Our job was easy. All we did was carry him. He put this Roofer team together. He organized, talked, cajoled. He encouraged, pushed, advised, listened. He listened hard. He laughed. He prayed. He connected us all to one another. We just carried him to the roof and pulled apart the tiles and lowered him down. There. Is that what you want?

And Wells moves aside. The Lord smiles on us. And Wells is running again.

After the Mass, the gathering of friends walked into the early evening, and we made our way to a pedestrian bridge that crossed the Spokane River. It was a spot Wells could see from his bedroom. We gathered around his two daughters as they tenderly poured—lowered—his cremated remains into the water. In a wonderful way, we were all Roofers once more. And looking down into the river, we knew and were known by the Christ who called to us in the sacred ritual of burying our brother.

I think that the image of the Roofers can be a great clarifying metaphor for the church. It drives to the heart of what I live and do on the streets of Portland, with my companions who are also committed to a life of service. We are Roofers. Roofers are broken open by their acts of love. Our focus—our obsession—is on the wounded brother or sister. The church discovers the love and truth and compassion of its heart in the service of the broken. Driven by love, it cannot get stuck in its selfishness, and it is dispossessed of the temptation to seek honor and riches and power. As Roofers, the church finds Christ whether it is nursing the AIDS patient or developing programs that will eliminate the causes of poverty or listening to the grief of a prison inmate. As Tony, the lead Roofer, might say, it is in the act of service that the church "discovers what it's all about," which is to say, in service it is gracefully drawn to its true purpose and meaning: to meet and be Christ in the world.

chapter thirteen

THE PEARLS OF MY LIFE:

WHAT KEEPS ME GOING

The pearls of my life are what I treasure the most, what I am willing to pay the price for, what I bet my life on, what I count as the greatest gifts of my life.

Again, the kingdom of heaven is like a merchant looking for fine pearls; when he finds one of great value he goes and sells everything he owns and buys it.
MATTHEW 13:45–46

In the end, after all this has been said, what keeps me going? How have I decided to keep chasing my dreams for human beings and the poor and not wound up chasing my tail? Where have I found the strength that we all need to live out our vocation in life?

It was Camus who said that we all work with three or four significant images in our lives. One of mine is the pearl. It is my favorite jewel. It requires time in its creation, forming microscopic layer after microscopic layer. Its beauty enhances all that surrounds it and the person who wears it. It wins me over with its lustrous nature, its delicate surface color, its dignity, simplicity, clarity, and directness. The pearl invites me to come and hold it and appreciate its wonder. It summons my tenderness. It fills me with a desire to hold it in my hand and next to my heart. It offers a delicate and powerful metaphor that helps to explain my life of love and service. The pearl, suffused with the meaning I give to it, becomes an inner icon for me, wherein I can treasure the truth of my life. It gives an answer to the questions I ask.

THE PEARL OF THE HEART OF GOD

It was you who created my inmost self,
and put me together in my mother's womb;
for all these mysteries I thank you:
for the wonder of myself, for the wonder of your
   works.

PSALM 139:13–14

When I ask what is certain for me in life and death, knowing that everything else may be anchored in it, the answer is the love of God as known in the heart of Christ. I am uncertain of how God began to work in me or, for that matter, when—or, more bewilderingly, why. What I have realized, though, over the years, is that life makes no sense unless I recognize, like the psalmist, that God is the author of my contingent being and that I am caught up in the mystery of God's presence in my life and in the love of God's heart as seen in Jesus. I wind up humbled before the mystery of it all.

I am, honest to God, still amazed that I am a Jesuit priest. Yet the events of my life have served and affirmed my vocation. This is not the statement of someone drunk on new wine. I don't kid myself about this; I know I am not behind this movement in my heart. Indeed, like Elijah of the Old Testament, there are times when I have had enough and simply want to crawl under a bush and die (1 Kings 19:3–4). But in the end, I move to the heart of God in my life and am invited to fall back in love. Heart against heart.

The pearl of God's heart is constantly placed before me: in creation, in the sacred love and courage of human beings, in my most intimate moments of prayer, and every day as I move in and through and among the hearts described in these pages. This pearl of the heart of God has, in the words of Jeremiah, seduced me and overpowered me.

THE PEARL OF THE POOR

Every week for the last several years a colorful drawing of religious images has arrived in my mailbox. The drawings are done and placed there by a developmentally disabled woman who loves me as a child loves her father. The tools of her craft are an army of colored pencils, a handful of stencils, and a heart that won't stop. They are some of my most precious gifts, out of a cache of gifts I have received over the years from the least of the brothers and sisters I have served. Like any gift, they are expressions of care for and belief in me.

The pearl of the poor enhances me; it calls me to life. Like the Gospel's merchant, I am in search of a pearl of great price—the pearl of the poor—and my life is a testament to that search. This pearl, when I hold it, brings out an inner beauty in me. If I harp on the need for the church to be poor and among the poor, it is because I know that the church will discover that the poor are its best teachers.

A cabdriver once said to me, commenting on some street people trudging along a lonely street at 2 A.M., "Look at those damn trolls." As I got out of the cab, I told him that he should be around the "trolls" more, to learn of their truth telling, their sense of loyalty, their hardships. He ought to know that the poor of the streets laugh and cry. It was too bad, I told him, that he did not know the joy of the poor or the grief of the poor. Were he to know all these things about such extraordinary human beings, he would be a better man. I finished my conversation with him by saying that he was, from my perspective, a close-minded and bigoted person. I walked into the night thinking that the poor are jewels that he will never hold to his heart.

The pearl of the poor has helped me pass into a deeper conversion, to examine myself against the prevailing values that our culture holds out to me, and to see where I most authentically live out my heart. St. Ignatius wanted members of the Society of Jesus to be poor—and therefore to serve the poor—because he knew that in their midst we would learn what real detachment is, what freedom to respond to God can mean, what humility can do to our hearts, and how we can be transformed by an experience of deep reliance on God.

One of the poorest women I know, Jennifer, a crippled and blind SRO resident who lives on a few bucks a month and with the disappointment caused by her drug-dabbling kids, keeps telling me that she can see and walk and live because God is always with her. Nothing obscures her love of God.

THE PEARL OF COMMITTED COMPANIONS

One day, while I was talking with an OMB staff person about the problems of a client, she began to weep. It was the result of a bitter clash within her, between her longing for his wholeness and her awareness of his brokenness. She was being pulled in two directions. I took her into my arms, partly to ease her pain and partly because she was such an inspiration to me. I was moved by her devotion, her willingness to follow her convictions into the uncertain and often unrewarding life of service, and her determination to keep on loving in spite of hardships. Her conviction glistened like a pearl.

What person who does what this woman does has not been there? How I admire them and cherish them. I see them each day, serving in a variety of ways, dealing with the heartbreaking realities of the poor: frustration; violent transference; physical and mental sickness; rejection; police harassment; loneliness; hunger for food, friendship, and purpose; anger at God; boredom; unemployment; feelings of stupidity, fury, and fear; shame; abandonment.

And yet, what service agency staff person or community organizer hasn't been amazed by the resiliency of the poor, no matter where that person serves: in shelters, detox centers, emergency rooms, health clinics, women's drop-in centers, nonprofit restaurants, assisted-living facilities, hospitals, mental health agencies, rescue missions, Catholic Worker houses. The love and dedication of these workers is a pearl for me. They find strength in wounds, and their touch can make the dead walk. Being around them is one of my greatest sources of hope and understanding. They show me what it means to walk the talk of justice for all.

THE PEARL OF FRIENDS

Most people know the pearl of one person's love and friendship. As I reflect on the pearl of my friends, I think of the person who is the dearest of all to me and of how she has enriched my life. Surely our relationship is a pearl. It has been created over time and, for the most part, at considerable distance. It is the product of pain and struggle, joy and communication; it has captured my heart with its dignity and honesty; it has summoned my tenderness and wonder; it has been my strength in some of my worst moments.

Because of this love of my dearest friend, I have learned to love myself and to find the freedom to listen to God's invitation to me to follow God as a Jesuit priest. In her friendship I have experienced the friendship of God. From her I have learned to listen without being possessive, without imposing myself. If any relationship has taught me about the beauty of the pearls of God, of the poor, and of other human beings, it has been this one. There will always be an underlying sadness in this friendship, the pain of something incomplete, because of the distance between us. Only hope in God, as Kathleen Norris says, allows us to know and enjoy the depth of our intimacy at a distance.

One of the most poignant scenes of love and friendship occurs regularly at airports. I like to watch arriving people being greeted by their loved ones. The reunions are vivid and heartwarming: the searching for the beloved, the joy of recognition, the race to another's arms, and then the heart-pounding embrace. In the arms of our loved ones, after separation, the press of exile is not so great, and the whole world looks like home.

I remember getting off a plane one night in Toronto, totally devastated by the events of the previous week. One of my closest friends, a Canadian Jesuit, was there to pick me up, hold me in his arms, comfort me, and spend days walking and talking with me as I healed. We have known each other for thirty-five years and are more than blood brothers. He is a pearl of a man.

A woman friend who worked with me on the streets and at whose wedding I officiated is one of my dearest confidantes, a person who knows as much about me as anyone. She is a pearl of a woman.

These are individuals who cherish me as I cherish them.

Who can make it without friends? Not me. The pearl of my friends is one I count on and hold to my heart at all times. I know that I can always pull it out and gaze upon it and hold it and touch it. My friends call me to life; they affirm and support me in my work, they laugh at my dumb jokes, they hold me in their arms, they hear me out, they support me in ventures that they don't understand, they believe in me, they back me in crisis and hail me in success, they give meaning in sunlight and darkness, they reflect the divine presence to me, they confront me and tell me the truth, and they call when I least expect it to affirm their love of me. I couldn't give a figure to the number of times in Old Town that I have sat with a friend and we have comforted each other. I couldn't count the number of late-night phone calls I have had with a friend who has brought me back to life.

Like the merchant's pearl in the Gospel story, the pearls of my life are what I treasure the most, what I am willing to pay the price for, what I bet my life on, what I count as the greatest gifts of my life. These pages have described my search for and discovery of these pearls.

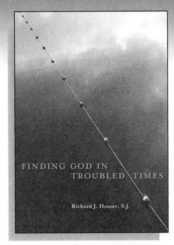